Countering the Conspiracy to Destroy Black Boys

Volume III

by Jawanza Kunjufu

African American Images
Chicago, Illinois

Cover Photo by Fela Kuumba
Cover Design by Eugene Winslow
Photo Credits: William Hall
First Edition   Fifth Printing
Copyright 1990 by Jawanza Kunjufu

Table of Contents

Preface

It was in 1982 when I first wrote *Countering the Conspiracy to Destroy Black Boys*. I had read and observed the plight of the African American man, but I became especially concerned with the development of Black boys. I've always been interested in attacking a problem before it starts, consequently the proper guidance of Black boys would reduce the problems we're experiencing with African American *men*. Volume I came as a result of witnessing a large number of African American boys in special education and lower tracked classes, along with a disproportionate number of suspensions. I've recommended that fourth grade was the most significant time for intervention.

Between 1982 and 1986, I had been asked numerous times "How can we counter this conspiracy", and to write more about it. Teachers and parents wanted more concrete ideas in hopes of reducing the number of African American boys being placed in special education classes. In 1986, I wrote Volume II that reviewed the relationship between mothers and their sons and the whole issue of responsibility. I offered the concept of how "mothers raise their daughters and love their sons". Teachers were given an understanding of the "showdown", the power struggle between female teachers and Black boys. A review of learning and teaching styles were provided in the hopes of reducing African American boys being placed in special education.

The Lord seems to inspire me every four years to write more about Black boys. There has been much progress since 1982 in response to African American males being on the endangered species list. Over a hundred organizations nationwide are conducting "Rites of Passage" programs. The concept of 100 Black Men is now in over twenty cities, giving boys positive role models. There have been numerous conferences, books and articles in the past decade keeping us abreast of the latest trends. Unfortunately, the problems have worsened since Volume II and so I write again. Over the past years the African American male prison population has increased. We now have 609,000 involved with the penal system while possessing only 436,000 in college. The prison population is 47 percent African American in contrast to 3.5 percent at the collegiate level.[1] Numerous studies project that 70 percent of all African American males will be unavailable to African American women by the year 2000.[2] These men will be dead, incarcerated, drug addicts, unemployed, mentally insane, homosexual, or involved in interracial marriages. The gangs and drug dealers have also become more effective over the past decade. The homicide rate is at an all-time high and the decline in employment opportunities makes drug dealing very lucrative for many of our youth.

My frustration is that we don't have a male shortage at birth through the elementary grades. There is no need for women to go without husbands and children to be denied fathers, if we intervene effectively.

In Volume III, I will dissect the developmental process of African American males by age. The age grouping will be infancy through nine, nine through thirteen, thirteen through eighteen, and eighteen through twenty-five. We must know what to look for in each group and make the necessary corrections. Please understand I use the word "we" often, because "I am" because "we are" and I could not do this by myself. "We" represents all the ancestors, scholars, staff, and family members, who have shaped me. Whatever, I have done in this world is attributed to a much larger body. To God be the Glory!

We must develop boys' fine motor skills in pre-school.

Chapter I

Infancy — Nine Years

I have grown tired over the years of hearing about the adult African American male shortage. Often times, the books, conferences, radio, and television specials, border on sensationalism. The topic has become good business. We seem to look at this issue only from a macro perspective and forget that the 17 to 20 million African American males each need to be viewed singularly under a microscope to determine what is needed to develop them into becoming responsible African American men. We have a minute shortage at birth. All the newborn African American girls born today statistically should have an ample number of men to choose from.

It is remarkable how the Lord works in the production of life. The chances of a sperm fertilizing an egg and developing through the entire birth cycle are one in a million. Unfortunately, in the African American community the chances of a successful birth are even more remote due to the lack of a pre- and postnatal care. The normal birth weight is 5.5lbs, but 13 percent of African American children are under weight in contrast to 6 percent for Whites. The infant mortality rate for African American children is 18 deaths per 1,000 live births in comparison to 9 for Whites. Black boys survive less than girls, 1,965 deaths per 100,000 live births versus girls at 1,603.1

The African American community resembles an underdeveloped country as it relates to the quality of care provided for expecting mothers and infants. In most large urban areas one tenth of all African American babies are addicted to drugs. Have you ever seen an adult withdraw from heroin or cocaine? The experience does not even compare to the trauma experienced by the infant whose first nine months were dependent on its substance. Seventy percent of all African American children are born out of wedlock. Female African American teenagers lead the industrialized world in teen pregnancy followed by Arab and Euro-Americans.

I often ask the Lord, if he would consider reversing the responsibility and allow the males to become pregnant. I was pleased to see Cosby allocate a show to this phenomenon. I honestly believe that this epidemic would subside in our community if the brothers got pregnant.

Would you
be more
careful
if it was you
that got
pregnant?

We would have birth control all over the town, similar to Europe if this were to happen. We need more programs like Project Alpha and Teen Fathers that stress that both male and female are responsible.

Frances Welsing suggests that to correct this problem in our race and to restore our people to their original greatness, we should delay marriage until the age of 28. She feels maturation would have taken place along with self-esteem. A couple should then wait until age 30 before having children; this will allow the couple to become better acquainted and discuss their views on childrearing (There are not too many things worse than to marry someone with different views on childrearing.). The couple should only have two children and spread them four years apart; this will allow adequate amount of individual nurturance and "lap time" before another child is born. Ironically, those with the *least* to give—time, money, nurturance, and direction, have the *most* children, and those with the *most* to give have the *least*. The future of our race depends on only bringing into the world children that are loved, nurtured, and given a sense of direction. Nation building is not based on *quantity*, but *quality*.

In contrast to Frances Welsings' theory of 28, 30, 2, and 4, in many of our communities, the rule of thumb has become 0, 13, 5 or more children and every nine months. We are not going to develop our race with that kind of lifestyle. From this point on, we will hone in on the specific problems and peculiarities that are affecting African American males. Many people are aware of the large disparity among African American males and females, as it relates to incarceration, homicide, suicide, alcoholism, and other ills. Most people are not aware that Black boys also lead Black girls in infant mortality as previously mentioned. Consequently, the male shortage has already begun (though many people think that the male shortage begins at age 18, 25, or 30.) When in actuality the male shortage begins at birth when there is a disproportionate number of Black boys that aren't able to survive birth. At the tender age of two weeks, a month, and three months, African American females already experience the Black male shortage.

3

The next period that we want to concentrate on is the preschool years. The period between six months and four to five years of age. This is a very important period. Many doctors and psychologists have pointed out that the brain's growth and development is greatest between infancy and three years of age, with the next greatest period being between three and six years of age. It becomes crucial that the African American community develop our children, especially our boys, during this critical period of brain development and cognitive growth. This area of child development is paramount in reinforcing fine motor and language development.

It becomes frightening when we have children that are addicted to drugs and are experiencing ramifications of becoming detoxified, as well as children who live in homes where fine and gross motor and language development is not encouraged. These are the reasons many people advocate the need for Homestart, Headstart, and other programs to develop these skills even before the child enters kindergarten. This reinforces the notion of professionals who advocate that this is the most prominent period between infancy and three, followed by three to five in child development. This is also the time when parents should be cradling their children close to them, placing toys that are in their range, but require movement to touch. Toys should be viewed as tools that are designed, not just for fun, but are also developmental. Many parents buy toys only for enjoyment and not for cognition. There is even an item called a cradle gym, where in the cradle tools can be placed to maximize development. It is remarkable how energetic and intelligent African American children are, especially if they are placed in environments with the proper nurturance, nutrition, and guidance that all children should receive.

There are numerous studies that have been done around the world contrasting and comparing what children have been able to do at certain stages. Listed below is a study that was done by several doctors comparing African and European American children and their ability to recognize stimuli and respond to it.

1. Nine hours old, being drawn up into a sitting position, able to prevent the head from falling backwards (Euro.-6 wks).
2. Two days old, with head held firmly, looking at face of the examiner (Euro.-8 wks).
3. Seven weeks old, supporting herself in a sitting position and watching her reflection in the mirror (Euro.-20 wks).
4. Five months old, holding herself upright (Euro.-nine months). Taking the round block out of its hole in the form board (Euro.-11 months).
5. Five months old, standing against the mirror (Euro.9-months).
6. Seven months old, walking to the Gesell Box to look inside (Euro.-15 months).
7. Eleven months old, climbing the steps alone (Euro.-15 months).[3]

These studies are very significant because if we really want to measure natural and raw intelligence, this would be the best time to do it, between infancy and three years of age. From that point on, we're really measuring what children have been exposed to, not intelligence. It becomes discouraging that our children, at a very young age have demonstrated a tremendous amount of intelligence only to place last on high school culture tests. The above indicators of innate intelligence points out that in the first three years, African American children are exceptional. Psychologists and educators have always recommended the need for parents to talk, read, and play games with their children. This will help their growth and development.

In dissecting this first stage of growth and development in Black males from infancy to nine years of age, there are two major components that I want to analyze. One is the dichotomy between fine motor and gross motor development, and the second is the issue of hyperactivity.

In looking at the first area, fine motor and gross motor development and trying to compare males and females. The female body on the average is 23 percent muscle, the male is 40 percent muscle.[4] Schools value fine motor development more than gross motor development, whether this is right or wrong. How well a child can hold a pencil, a crayon, or a pair of scissors (fine motor) is valued more than their ability to hold a ball, play with a truck, grab an object, and wrestle with one another (gross motor). Many families early on can be found making the statement, "boys will be boys", and will have two young children at home. The daughter will be coloring and the boy will be playing with his truck, car, or basketball. This is a very complicated point; are we saying that we want to take gross motor objects away from Black boys and force them at the tender age of two and three to sit still with crayons, pencils, and scissors? Are we saying that we should take the pencils and pens and scissors away from girls and give them trucks, balls, and large gross motor objects to manipulate? Or, are we suggesting that schools find other ways to measure learning besides a left brain, analytical, fine motor approach. Schools must realize that intelligence can be measured in other ways besides pencil and paper. All these factors need to be considered, but ultimately what we are trying to do is develop Black boys into men.

The first step in achieving this is not to compare boys to girls, and assume that boys are deficient. Diane McGuinness has written an excellent book on the subject, *When Children Don't Learn*. Many people have often wondered, are boys and girls different. While we have some general feelings about differences, how do we allow for those differences in preschool programs, kindergarten, primary, intermediate, and upper grades? It becomes very concerning when 75 percent of all people that are dyslexic are male, 90 percent of the children labeled hyperactive are male, and 75 percent of children in remedial reading are male.[5] This applies to both Black and White males.

Some how we have this general sentiment that boys and girls are different. Yet we have not allowed for those differences in the home and in the classroom, so that both boys and girls can develop. If we define growth and development from a female perspective, ie. how long you can sit still, or how well you can hold a pencil, crayon, or pair of scissors, then we may be defining success that will be detrimental to male growth and development. Diane McGuinness points out in her book, that there is a relationship between reading and hearing. Studies have confirmed that in order to read, you have to be able to hear the syllables. Females' hearing abilities are greater than males.

The response of the human ear at auditory threshold has maximum sensitivity of about 1,000 cycles per second (cps). This is approximately "high C" in the musical scale. Hearing becomes less and less efficient both above and below this frequency, until all sounds become completely inaudible below 20 cps and above 20,000 cps, which is the limit of human hearing. When we get older or expose our ears to very loud sounds, such as factory noise or rock music, the upper range of hearing deteriorates.

When the sexes are compared, females show a greater sensitivity at threshold for sounds above 3,000 cycles, and their sensitivity relative to males improves at higher frequencies. The sex differences become more pronounced with age, and women suffer much less hearing loss than men. Females were found to have greater sensitivity above 3,000 cps. I have found very similar results on a population of fifty college students. These results help us to understand part of the females' advantage in the development of language, because high-frequency sensitivity is particularly important in the accurate perception of certain speech sounds, especially the consonants c, s, t, x, and z.

In tests of comfortable loudness the sex differences are perhaps the greatest. I asked fifty British college students to increase the volume of sound until it became "just too loud." The women set considerably lower levels of volume than the men across a broad range of frequencies. The difference between the sexes

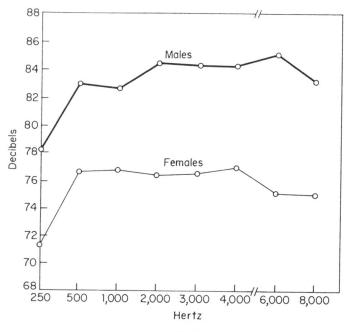

FIGURE 5.1

was a constant 7 to 8 decibels across the entire frequency range (see figure 5.1).[6]

Later on in the chapter as we move into the primary grade period between kindergarten and third grade, we will discuss this research in more detail and its implications on reading abilities. As for now, we are looking at the period between six months and three to four years of age. We are looking at the fine and the gross motor skills and language development of our children as it relates to the home.

It becomes imperative that schools acknowledge that males and females mature at different levels. Research indicates that girls mature about two years ahead of boys. Unless schools are willing to make some adjustments in evaluating and labeling children, then the only alternative is for parents to accept female expectations about their male children. Parents can try to accelerate their son's growth and development by greater utilization of fine motor objects and strengthening their hearing abilities by reading to them and reducing loud music, especially loud rap music which, also impairs hearing in young Black boys.

Two schools of thought developed on this dilemma came from Maria Montessori, a medical doctor and Alfred Binet, a psychologist. Binet took the approach of developing a test that was unfortunately used to classify children; even he acknowledged that the test should be used as an indicator and not for classification. Many educators like classifying children. Some people feel comfortable when they can put children into categories. This comes out of a left-brain school of thought where there is a need to place people and objects into divisions.

I've always marveled when people have tried to make Nancy Wilson and Wynton Marsalis choose what category of music that they sing and play. They consistently say, "I am a singer and musician. I'll perform while you classify". The same approach takes place in our schools.

The Montessori approach realized that children develop at different rates; (males and females, and ethnic groups) and that there's nothing wrong with children developing or learning at different rates, or in different styles. We should design homes and classrooms to allow for those differences and to encourage children to express themselves in ways that are comfortable. Unfortunately, the Montessori approach is least used in our schools and classification dominates. As a result, a high number of male children are labeled hyperactive and dyslexia, then placed in remedial reading classes and ultimately special ed.

The second area that I want to look at is hyperactivity. The energy level of African American children is referred to by some psychologists as verve. The word hyperactive is a value judgement. The word is based on an assumption that we have an understanding and knowledge of what is normal activity. It may not be that African American children and specifically African

9

American male children are hyperactive. It may be that the stimuli around them simply is not challenging enough. They choose to become involved with other activities that are of interest to them.

There was a study done by Ohio State, looking at two very popular television shows, Mr Rogers and Sesame Street. Mr. Rogers is a very slow moving show, Sesame Street is more action oriented. The images change more frequently. Yale University found that African American children responded better to Sesame Street and European American children responded better to Mr. Rogers.[7] Unfortunately, the classroom moves at a pace similiar to the Mr. Rogers' show. Therefore, it may not be that African American children, and specifically African American male children are hyperactive. It may be that the methodology is simply too slow. Interesting enough, boys of all races do not seem to be hyperactive when they play video games or when involved in other activities that capture their interest.

Shown in the two figures below are results of a study measuring children's interest level in various activities, which reinforces that hyperactivity may not be the issue. What children are involved with will determine their interest level. We may need to look at the stimuli we provide for children rather than label children hyperactive when they do not respond as we deem appropriate.

Figure 9.1 illustrates the scores for the average duration in minutes for each of these categories. Perseverance, for example, was calculated as the longest time a child spent on any one activity during the period of the observation. The average time for the girls was twelve minutes, for the boys, eight minutes. Girls spent twice as much time in play organized by the teacher (usually, but not always, female), whereas males spent twice as much time in unsupervised play—constructing things or watching other children.

Figure 9.2 illustrates the frequency of occurrence of certain behaviors. Boys are found to carry out four and one-half different activities in twenty minutes, girls only two and one-half.

Figure 9.1

HYPERACTIVITY: A Diagnosis in Search of a Patient

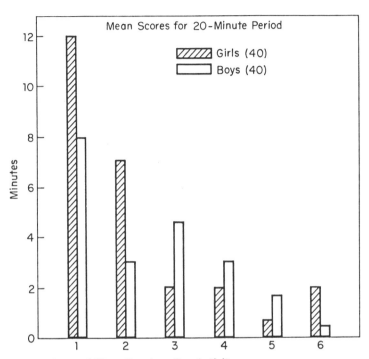

1 – Longest Time Spent on One Activity
2 – Time Spent in Teacher Organized Activity
3 – Time Spent in Construction-Toy Play
4 – Time Spent Watching Others
5 – Longest Time Watching Others
6 – Time Spent Painting Alone

Particularly interesting is the number of interruptions of on-going play. Boys interrupted what they were doing three times more frequently than girls. Behaviors in categories 7 to 9, which were intended to tap destructive and aggressive behaviors, occurred extremely infrequently. None of our observers ever saw any serious misbehavior, and no child at this excellent pre-

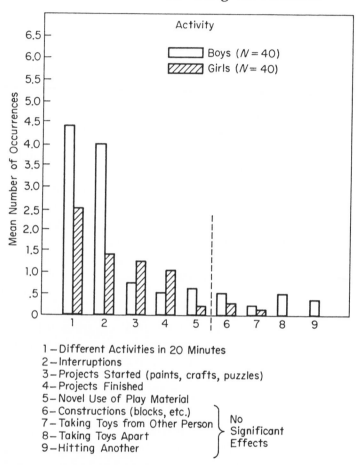

Figure 9.2

HYPERACTIVITY: Unraveling the Evidence

1 – Different Activities in 20 Minutes
2 – Interruptions
3 – Projects Started (paints, crafts, puzzles)
4 – Projects Finished
5 – Novel Use of Play Material
6 – Constructions (blocks, etc.)
7 – Taking Toys from Other Person
8 – Taking Toys Apart
9 – Hitting Another

} No Significant Effects

school was considered deviant, hyperactive, or difficult to control. Therefore, a sex difference of the magnitude we discovered is all the more remarkable and illustrates that when children are left to their own devices, "boys time their actions differently from girls". In a classroom setting, the routine and structure favors the timing patterns of girls far more so than that of boys. Imposing these unnatural temporal constraints on young boys can disrupt their normal rhythms and produce frustration and tension.[8]

The African American home is filled with a great degree of stimuli. Many psychologists and social workers who have not lived or been trained in the African American experience label the African American home as chaotic. A home that has five or more children, two or three radios playing at the same time on different stations, extended family members entering and leaving the home is for many educators, psychologists, and social workers quite overwhelming. Children that come out of these kinds of homes have developed an ability to do more than one task at the same time. They are more people than object oriented and prefer interacting with children than objects. A child being raised in a home with none or only one sibling performing only one task at a time, only doing homework where there is quiet, is geared more toward the American classroom. Again, we are faced with a dilemma.

Schools will need to understand that children with higher energy levels are not hyperactive, but simply have a higher verve. The level of intelligence demonstrated by African children during infancy confirms that innate talent exists and schools should be charged with creating an environment that maximizes cognition with classifications. I and so many others are doing all that we can to provide in-service training to teachers to better understand the relationship between culture and learning styles. People and institutions move very slowly. Or, we have to place pressure on African American homes to reduce the stimuli. Parents with children in this critical stage, between infancy and five years of age may need to match the American classroom with the African American home. I stated earlier that we may need to reduce the trucks, basketballs, and large gross motor objects that are given to our boys and increase the number of fine motor tools boys need to be involved with, in preparation for kindergarten and the primary grades.

We also recommend that the African American homes reduce the music. Many teachers have indicated that there is simply no quiet time at home and their classroom is not going to teach reading with "Public Enemy" and "Boogie Down Productions" playing in the background. From three o'clock to nine o'clock there is a greater degree of noise in many of our homes. It becomes imperative if we are going to reduce the number of African American children, and specifically African American male children from being hyperactive, then parents and teachers must compromise. Parents need to institute quiet time where children are expected to sit still for a few minutes. As they become older, teachers have greater expectations on the number of minutes they can sit still, playing games such as "Concentration" and "Simon Says" enhances listening skills and following directions. These are problems teachers say are acute to African American boys. Parents can cultivate their male child's development by reading and discussing ideas together. This interaction will give you an opportunity to evaluate personally your child's development.

We must also develop our children's social skills. They must be taught manners and respect for authority. When children enter pre-school, kindergarten, and primary grades, teachers are very concerned about children's social skills. They observe how well children interact with one another, and are they respectful and cooperative with each other.

Many teachers feel that African American boys are very aggressive. It's crucial that parents teach their boys social skills, manners, and a respect for authority. There is an African proverb, that says, "It takes a *whole* village to raise *a* child, not a single parent or two parents—a village. Unfortunately, many African American parents are telling their children, "You don't have to respect anybody but me". As a result, children at a young age are telling their teachers, neighbors, and other adults, "You're not my mama, you can't tell me what to do". One of the major strengths of the Asian child, besides being obedient, exhibiting discipline, and valuing education, is their respect for authority, which means respect for their elders. African American boys may have the greatest problem in respecting authority figures.

The aggression being expressed in the classroom, to their own demise, contributes heavily to being placed in special ed classes.

We as parents have to ask ourselves, "Have we given our boys the resources necessary to have a successful academic and social experience? We have to ask ourselves as educators, "Are we going to provide a fair opportunity for boys in the classroom without comparing them to girls, European American and Asian-American children? Have we provided the experience and the environment that will allow boys to grow to their fullest potential?

Now we face the next hurdle, kindergarten. Children, specifically African American male children are failing. It has now reached an epidemic level, where you can now fail kindergarten. This was unheard of 10, 15, 20 years ago. The self-esteem of a child failing kindergarten is greatly affected. From this point on in their educational career, he/she will be one year behind everyone else. He/she will have to explain to the other children every year why the age and the grade do not correspond.

The National Association of Educating Young Children (NAEYC) has gone on record trying to appeal to educators that we should not compare children, especially when some children were involved in a formal educational experience as early as six months of age to a child whose first formal experience was kindergarten. Kindergarten teachers cannot determine what children are bringing to them. Teachers should take children as they are and develop them based on the curriculum that was designed at the kindergarten level.

Is it fair to a child who was not taught his numbers, alphabets, and colors before the first day of kindergarten, to be placed in the slowest group and labeled at risk? Kindergarten used to be the grade where children were introduced to colors, alphabets, numbers, the spelling of their names, social skills, and fine motor skills. Due to the wide disparity in income levels and other social economic factors, many parents have prepared their children before kindergarten with some of these skills. Rather than accepting this, educators negatively evaluate

15

children that are not exposed to these learning skills, and have already begun tracking at the kindergarten level.

Many parents and community people in large urban areas ponder the reasons for the high dropout rate of 50 percent and upward. Children can be in the 9th grade and read on a 3rd through 5th grade level (a wide disparity among students exists in the same class). The difference begins before children entered into the formal kindergarten experience. I'm appealing to African American parents to expose their children to the kinds of experiences they are going to be expected to master in kindergarten. It is also an opportunity for teachers and educators to again assess whether they're providing an opportunity that is fair to all children. Whatever academic achievement levels that existed between one child and another before kindergarten *widens* with their educational experience because of tracking. Tracking begins as early as the eighth day of kindergarten according to Ray Rist in an article in the Harvard Educational Review.[9]

First, how much academic information does a teacher have on a child on the eighth day of kindergarten? They have very little. They relied on the social workers' interview and the parental registration form. They also look at how children were dressed, the way they smelled, were they verbal with adults, did they speak black english, was a father in the home, were they low income, and what was their energy level in the classroom. Children that did not meet the teacher's feminine, middle class standards were placed in the lowest reading group. The study goes on to point out that the children in the lowest reading group received the lowest level of expectations. The study, which was a longitudinal study, also demonstrated that the same children evaluated as early as the eighth day of kindergarten that were placed in the highest reading group remained there throughout the first and second grade and those in the lower grade did also. This initial classification has now become a self-fulfilling prophecy. If this format continues throughout the primary, intermediate, and upper grades, we're going to see a large differential which was created by "at risk schools" not "at risk children".

Because we are interested in the unique features and characteristics, and issues that are germane to the African American male child, lets look at some of the differences between African American males and females, and males and females in general, in the kindergarten through third grade experience.

African American children are 17 percent of public school children in this nation, but they constitute 41 percent of the children placed in special ed. The first concern, why the disproportion in numbers of African American children in special ed? We believe that any number greater than 17 is excessive. The problem gets compounded when 85 percent of the time it's the African American male child. We believe that any number beyond 50 percent is also too high and that before we look at the boys, we have to look at educators and the school environment and ask ourselves, "What is it about the environment and our assessment tools that promotes the placing of Black boys in special ed more than Black girls, and placing African American children in special ed more than European American children?

If the ideal student is a female, wears a yellow dress, quiet, cooperative, and attempts to please the teacher, and in contrast, if the African American boy wears jeans, is aggressive, possesses a high energy level and does not always cooperate with teachers, does that dictate that boys of all races deserve to be 90 percent of the children labeled hyperactive, 75 percent of the children placed in remedial reading, and 85 percent of the children placed in special ed?

The problem is further compounded when many people do not value statistics and only acknowledge personal experiences. If we have a class of 30 students, consisting of 15 males and females, and five of the male students are labeled special ed, we can look at this situation in one of two ways: We can either say the problem is with the five boys and their behavior because the other 10 boys did not have this same problem, or we say that when you have one third of your males negatively classified we need to re-assess our measurement tools.

We have two boys in our class, the first boy's name is Darryl. He is very quiet, non athletic, cooperative, and fearful of strangers. The other kindergarten student is Richard, he's athletic, very talkative, and popular. Darryl, by most teachers' standards will be a good student while Richard will be viewed with suspect. If we only value academic intelligence to the exclusion of social, kinetics, athletic, spatial, and musical intelligence, then Richard could also be intelligent.

Another example, we have four levels of students: Low income, middle income, White, and Black students. The teacher reads the children a story. The middle and lower income White students, and middle income African American students regurgitate the story back to the teacher exactly as it was read. Rote learning and memorization is taking place. The lower income Black students jazzed it up. They brought in some additional characters, put in a little body movement, made it more interesting, original, convincing, and dramatic. If we only value rote learning, three groups receive an A, and the last group fails. If we also value being original, dramatic, and convincing, then the last group would also receive an A.

Unfortunately, in most American schools the last group would not have received an A because we only measure intelligence and academic achievement in very narrow parameters. If African American children cannot perform within those dimensions then they are labeled in ways that literally determine their future.

Earlier, I mentioned in the chapter that there are physical differences between males and females. Whether we look at the development of muscles, hearing abilities, or the overall maturation rate of boys and girls, there are differences. The question is, do we allow for those differences in the classroom? It is obvious from the statistics, that we have done a very poor job of acknowledging the differences in males and females and in Afri-

18

cans and Europeans.

The factors that contribute to this, exceed racism. Sexism is a part of it. When 83 percent of your teaching staff is female, 92 percent of your teaching staff is White, and only 1.2 percent of your teaching staff is African American male, it is a very good chance that the group that's least represented, (African American males) are going to receive the brunt of the improper or inappropriate labeling that's taking place in our school system. A whole book could be written on the relationship between female teachers and African American male students. In my earlier book, *Critical Issues in Educating African American Youth*, I indicated that the most important factor for the growth and development of children is not the *race* or the *gender* of the teacher but his/her *expectations*. I maintain that position. This does not negate my concern about the relationship between White female teachers and Black male students. This relationship has the greatest misunderstanding and lack of bonding, and yet it is a very popular occurrence and it's going to increase as the number of African American teachers decline.

Males and females learn in different ways; they mature at different levels. White boys also suffer from this education system, but because of a world based on White male supremacy, a White boy with a high school diploma will receive more money than a White or Black female, or Black male with a college degree. Black boys are not as fortunate to have a father who may own a corporation or benefit from White male privilege.

The remedies for this problem of trying to reduce the number of Black boys in remedial reading, special ed and being hyperactive is for schools to realize that children learn differently, for parents to establish quiet time, introduce fine motor activities, to teach respect for authority figures, and improve social grace. In addition to the previous cited solutions, we will also introduce or develop the notion of an all Black male classroom, a classroom consisting of only Black boys being taught by a Black male teacher. This solution would remove the opportunity to compare boys and girls, therefore boys will not be faced with the pressures of having to act like girls, if that's considered the ideal student. The next chapter will describe the procedures of this class. Another possibility is to delay boys entry into kindergarten by one or two years because of the maturation difference. In this way we will not have a five year old boy competing with a five year old girl. Obviously, these two are not ideal solutions.

Ideally, we need an educator who recognizes that children learn in different ways. We cannot accept the high disproportionate number of Black boys being placed in special ed; either we make the adjustments or we implement these extreme solutions because we have severe problems.

The recommendation of starting boys one to two years later to encompass the fact that girls mature about two years ahead of boys could be offset if schools, when classifying children, would consider gender differences. For example, boys may not be behind in reading if we only compared males to males, rather than comparing male scores to all students. Males may be two years behind girls in reading but may not be two years behind each other. In this context, if a girl was two years behind female students, then those girls would go into remedial reading along with all boys that are also two years behind male students. This way, we will be comparing apples to apples.

It may not be that boys are poor readers; it may be that boys simply mature and develop reading skills slower than girls. Studies also point out that because boys are more spatially and visually developed, which again may indicate their interest in playing videos, that boys are more advanced in mathematical skills, especially higher order mathematics, geometry, and trigonometry, because it relies more on spatial and visual development.

In Volume I, of *Countering the Conspiracy to Destroy Black Boys*, I indicated the fourth grade syndrome; the scores of boys decline from the fourth grade. We will be looking at that in more detail in the next chapter. In this chapter, I want to point out that we have more teachers who realize that children have different learning styles than we do at any other grade level. The primary teacher, kindergarten through third grade, provides more of a wholistic learning approach than any other group. My interest is for teachers, fourth through 12th grade, to also realize that children learn in different ways.

It is in the primary division that teachers use less ditto sheets and use the oral traditions, pictures, fine arts, and artifacts. It is from the fourth grade on, that we use more of a left-brain, written, analytical approach to teaching children. I wish we had more primary grade teachers teaching at the upper grades who would use those same five areas to present a lesson, especially to the African American male child who often prefers learning in other ways. It is in the primary grade that you see children involved in drawing, music, drama, and other modes of learning.

This book is an attempt to develop Black boys into men by reviewing four age categories. This first chapter has been infancy to nine. The male shortage that we hear so much about is very small at this first level. At this initial level, we are experiencing two problems: infant mortality is disproportionately higher for males than females. The second one is that schools, not understanding that males and females mature at different levels have already begun the negative classification of males, specifically African American male children. The shortage will now magnify.

There is a relationship between the excessive number of Black boys in special education and the 609,000 African American males that are involved in the penal system. Our concern is that we can intervene as early as infancy, if parents and teachers heed to the suggestions previously offered.

Throughout the book, we will be using barometers that we would like for parents, teachers, and community people to monitor. We need to have some mechanism to evaluate how well our boys are doing. The barometers that we will use throughout the book will be how well boys have developed themselves spiritually, in relationship to God. Secondly, their commitment, understanding, and appreciation of their race, that is, their African identity. Third, their level of scholarship;

their academic achievement level, especially in the area of reading and test taking. Fourth, will be their level of self-esteem. Fifth will be their respect for their parents and other adults. Sixth will be the amount of time they spend with their friends, and its influence on their values. Seventh will be their level of responsibility for their behavior and their actions. Lets review these seven barometers; spirituality, racial awareness, scholarship, self-esteem, respect for parents and elders, peer pressure, and responsibility. We don't have to wait until boys are 18 to find out if they are in trouble. We can find out during this stage with these seven areas.

In the first category, spirituality, there are studies that point out that little boys that were reared in Sunday School have less chance of going to prison. I like that kind of research. We hear so much about what the church is not doing. I think it is very interesting how going to Sunday School can reduce the possibilities of going to prison. I think it's also important to recognize that even children that are reared in the church and leave when they become older, often return back to the church, if for no other reason than that's where they were raised.

In this first barometer, we are in trouble if a large number of children, specifically male children, are not developing spiritually. In a later chapter we will even look at how parents have different expectations for whether their son or daughter will go to church. The relationship with God will reduce the homicide and self-hatred that exist in the African American community.

Secondly, how are children developing in their African consciousness and awareness? I believe that we can develop Black boys to be men, if we have African American boys that can bond and identify and understand the life of Malcolm X and Martin Luther King, Jr., have a vision of their history, that goes beyond 1619, and can visualize Imhotep designing the first pyramid. I believe our boys are "at risk" when they have a negative image of their history.

The third area was scholarship. We can measure the growth and development of boys by their reading level. It is essential that boys are taught how to read. It is imperative that we improve the hearing level of our boys and that we use the phonetic approach to reading which teaches children to attack a word and break it into syllables. We need to provide them with reading materials that are culturally relevant and will enhance their interest. It is also important that adults be mindful that America is a test-taking country, and African American boys must master test-taking skills.

Self-esteem was the fourth category. In later chapters we are going to provide a comparison study between *self*-esteem and *school*-esteem. Many educators will have us to believe that our boys have low self-esteem. It may not be that boys have low self-esteem, it may be that because they are placed in classrooms where they are slower than the girls, (remedial reading) lower track classes or special ed, the schools destroy the boys' self-esteem. In all the others endeavors and activities, playing sports, listening to rap music, and other social activities, our boys have a high level of self-esteem.

This is a very important area we need to monitor; children's self-esteem, but more specifically, the school-esteem because its a major factor in their growth and development. We cannot allow boys to simply withdraw from academics out of frustration and apply themselves and gain confidence in how well they fight, play basketball, and make rap records. It is obvious that it may not be our children's low self-esteem, but the environment and the insensitivity of educators to the African American male students.

Schools often have me speak to the male students with the major premise being that the boys lack self-esteem. I take the opposite opinion, that our boys came into the classroom at kindergarten with a very high level of self-esteem and the teacher's low expectations, and the lack of understanding the male child and his learning styles, destroyed it. We need to monitor our childrens' self-esteem throughout their academic career.

The fifth indicator of how well we are doing in developing

boys into men would be the amount of time they spend with their friends and their influence on their decisions. Studies indicate that the greatest influence on children is the peer group, followed by television, home, school, and church. Studies also show that home was number one followed by school, church, peer pressure, and television.[10] How well African American families can reduce the amount of time children spend with their friends and its influence on their decisions will also determine how well we develop boys.

The sixth area, is teaching Black boys to respect parents and elders. It was mentioned earlier that it takes a whole village to raise a child, we have a lot of youths, especially male youths, that are not respecting their parents. In the third chapter, we will look at the period between 13 and 18 years of age, (adolescence); we have a lot of boys who, not only do not respect their teachers and adults, but their mothers as well. You have mothers who then say, "I don't know what to do with him". This loss of control did not begin at 13, it began very early. It may have begun in this first period, infancy through nine. There are parents who have lost control of their boys before the age of nine. Many parents, especially mothers nag their boys, negotiate with their boys; have discussions about when they should wash dishes and when they should empty the garbage and then wonder, how they lost control of their boys. Most believe they lost him when he became a teenager, when they may have lost him before nine. We are very concerned about this area of our children's growth and development and we have to instill respect for elders in our boys.

Lastly, the area of responsibility, it has often been said that we have a lot of irresponsible men. You cannot be an irresponsible man unless you were allowed to be irresponsible as a boy. Teenage pregnancy is running rampant and 90 percent of the programs are geared for females and let the males off the hook. So the question becomes, who is going to teach Black boys to be responsible? You don't start at 16, when he's already made a baby. You start very early.

We need parents to teach boys to be responsible for their hygiene, clothes, rooms, and chores. Throughout the book, we look at other areas of responsibilities, but we believe that early on at the tender age of two, three, and four we need parents that will teach boys to be responsible in some basic areas and then we will expand upon that as boys continue to develop and grow.

In the second chapter, we will now look at the period between nine and thirteen. I feel that this is the most significant period in Black boys' growth and development. We call this the Fourth Grade Syndrome.

The fourth grade is the most pivotal time in the African American male development.

Chapter 2

Preadolescent (nine through thirteen)

In this book we are looking at various stages in the development of Black boys. The four stages are: infancy through nine, 9 through 13, 13 through 18, and 18 through 25. I believe that the most important period during the growth and development of Black boys is the period between 9 and 13. The most important stage is when boys are nine years of age and in the fourth grade.

In *Countering the Conspiracy to Destroy Black Boys*, Vol. 1, we identified a public school that met all the demographics, income level, family size, and educational attainment. We wanted to look at a school where Black boys attended the same school from fourth grade through eighth grade to measure their progress. Listed below is a chart showing the achievement level of Black boys at the beginning of the third grade and the end of the seventh.

I am not saying that the problem of Black boys began in the fourth grade. In the earlier chapter, I indicated the concerns start with a lack of prenatal care and the use of drugs during pregnancy. Regardless of that and inspite of all the other factors that took place between infancy and nine, I think the age of nine is the most pivotal.

There was a research study commissioned in New Orleans by the Public School system lead by Antoine Garibaldi that reviewed the problems facing Black boys.[1] This study shows the

Beginning Third Grade Percentile	Ending Seventh Grade Percentile	Reading Progress (Years)
98	35	1.3
97	54	2.7
92	24	2.1
91	68	3.1
81	72	3.9
72	72	3.6
66	59	3.9
63	7	.7
63	4	0
57	39	3.2
47	9	2.1
41	11	2.5
29	12	3.0
21	44	5.6
21	29	4.7
21	17	3.8
18	1	1.3
16	39	4.6
7	30	4.5
5	5	3.2_2

problem starting very early; this does not negate my concern about the fourth grade. We are simply saying that looking at the graph, that Black boys, inspite of the harsh problems they experience, do reasonably well. The above graph indicates that scores decline with each passing grade. The objective in this chapter is to analyze the factors that are taking place in the lives of Black boys between the ages of nine and thirteen, and what we can do to circumvent them.

The significance of this research lies in the area of public policy and intervention. There is a limited amount of human and financial resources. It becomes paramount that all programs are designed to be cost effective. Presently the U.S. government will allocate between $18,000 and $38,000 to send someone to prison, $2,300 to Headstart, and $10,000 to send someone to a public college. What is unfortunate is that 85 percent of inmates released from prison return; yet all kinds of studies, reinforce that Headstart, Chapter One and college are effective. If we are serious about solving the problems facing Black boys, then I think we need to understand *when* is the best time to intervene.

As a national consultant to school districts, one of the workshops I enjoy giving the most is entitled: Factors that Contribute to the Fourth Grade Syndrome. I strongly believe that only when we understand what is taking place in the lives of African American boys at the age of 9 will we then rectify it. The factors that contribute to the decline in African American boys' achievement are:

- A decline in parental involvement.
- An increase in peer pressure.
- A decline in nurturance and an increase in discipline problems.
- A decline in teacher expectations.
- A lack of understanding of learning style.
- A lack of male teachers.

Let's review the above factors.

As the age increases parental involvement decreases. I don't know who told parents that when children become older they need less of our time rather than more. When I speak to Headstart parents across the country, 80 percent of them are present. At the elementary school level it declines to 30 percent and in most high schools, parent meetings aren't even considered.

My wife and I have two sons 18 and 13, We believe that the 18 year old son needs us more than the 13 year old. We need parents that will remain involved in their son's growth and development, from infancy through 18. It bothers me that we have so many parents who will attend their children's graduation and such a small number attend PTA meetings. I call these graduation parents. Can you imagine instituting a rule that stated, you can only attend the graduation based upon the number of PTA meetings you attended.

The next factor is the direct relationship between age and peer pressure. For most children, peer pressure has become the number one influence in their lives, exceeding the influence of their parents, teachers, and ministers. There are several factors for this. Unfortunately, the major reason is that our children spend more time with their peers than with parents, teachers, and ministers. They also want to look and act like their friends and that's why role models, especially adult Black male role models are so important. Mothers have often told me that I can say the exact same thing to their son that they've said to them and it means more coming from a Black man. My children have also shared with me that their friends have made similiar comments to mine and it means more coming from their friends. Most children emulate people that look like them.

Many people think that all peer pressure is negative. Peer pressure in and of itself is not negative; only when the peer group *is not* reinforcing positive values does it become detrimental. It is the fusion of peer pressure, age, and street time that youth become socially aware of the contradictions between what schools teach and the realities of their communities.

I remember speaking at a school in Seattle, in the heart of the African American community. There were 41 White male pictures on the wall representing the 41 U.S. Presidents. This really bothered me, the lack of Black male pictures, but it seemed to be okay for the staff teaching these children. In contrast, those children would leave this school and go out into the real world where "Silky Floyd" and "Smooth Reggie" and other brothers are selling drugs or simply hanging on the corner waiting for life to give them a sense of direction. It is at this period that African American boys begin to wonder, "What is the relevance of learning that Columbus discovered America, Lincoln freed the slaves, and Hippocrates was the first doctor? What does this have to do with the survival of my community?" I advocate that children have the right to ask why they are learning a particular lesson. I don't think this request is one of defiance or belligerence; I simply feel that if children have to remain in school eight years for an elementary diploma, four years for a high school diploma, and four years for a bachelors degree, and additional years for a masters and Ph.D. then they deserve to have some input into what they are learning or at least question why it is important that they understand these concepts. I also feel that if we can't find some congruency between the lesson and the real world, then it's worth considering removing this from the curriculum.

The next factor that contributes to the fourth grade syndrome is the perception that our boys are no longer cute and innocent. To some, as they become older, they become more aggressive, hostile and a disciplinary problem. It is amazing to me how little Christopher at 3, 5 and 7 years of age could be viewed as a nice, sweet, innocent little boy, and now that Christopher has become 9, 11, and 13 he's viewed as being rough, rugged, and aggressive and now being recommended for suspension.

Many teachers and parents during the first period, between infancy through nine used their size to discipline. They simply were larger than the boys. From the fourth grade on, children, specifically most boys, become taller than teachers. They can look adults directly in the eye and as they become older they will probably look down at them. Teachers and parents will be unable to discipline male students with their height. For the insecure or intimidated parent or teacher, this becomes a serious dilemma to have a child look them in the eye and not back down. This situation requires a parent or teacher who is very confident and assertive. This is the kind of adult who gives very clear messages on who is in control in the classroom as well as in the home. This reminds me of the stories of the good old days when a four foot one mother who was seventy years of age could tell a seven foot 30 year old son, "I brought you in here and I'll take you out".

I am very much aware of the limitations that schools now have upon them about not being able to spank children, that's why I stress that adults who give very clear assertive messages are still effective in the classroom. Parents need to tell children that any adult that you come in contact with is to be respected. He/she is a member of the village.

31

The next area is lower teacher expectations. Numerous studies by Wilbur Brookeover, Ron Edmonds, and Antoine Garibaldi indicate that some teachers lower expectations based on the race, income, gender, and appearance of the child. For Black boys, the combination of being African American, male, low income, and poorly dressed makes them "at risk".

This is a very popular term, "at risk", most people that use the term look toward the victim. When we use the term, we need to look at the institutions and the factors that caused this child to be "at risk". The study that was done in New Orleans indicated that 60 percent of the teachers did not believe that African American boys were going to college. I reiterate that teacher expectations is the most important factor in academic achievement. You do not measure a school based upon facilities, nor who you sit next to, but who is in front of the class. I believe that what teachers *see* in the child is what they produce *out* of the child. If teachers see in Black boys future engineers, computer programmers, and doctors; if they see Benjamin Carson and Walter Massey, then they will produce those kinds of scholars.

Our research shows that children learn best when they are given feedback and reinforcement. Studies indicate that low achieving Black boys are given very few clues and feedback when answering a question incorrectly. Research indicates they receive approximately six seconds to correct a wrong answer, but when a high achieving student, specifically a female student answers a question incorrectly, she is given several clues, feedback and approximately three minutes to correct the wrong answer.[2] I believe that low achieving African American boys would also have answered the question correctly with this kind of prodding, nurturance, and attention.

In the fourth grade, more abstract thinking is expected. It becomes less child centered, more homework is allocated, and less movement is allowed in the classroom. There is more of a left-brain methodology conducted and less right-brain lesson plan, ie. stories, pictures, fine arts, and artifacts.

In the first period between infancy and nine, we indicated that boys have a slower maturation rate, are considered hyperactive, and disproportionately placed in remedial reading and special ed. The fourth grade and this whole intermediate period reminds me of the final decision on who's going to make the professional or varsity sports team. Can Black boys avoid the labels and remain on the team?

A whole book could be written on helping teachers to better understand African American children's learning styles, specifically Black boys. I strongly encourage the reader to read Volume II of *Countering the Conspiracy to Destroy Black Boys*, where I attempted to provide this for teachers of Black male students. Janice Hale Benson's book, *Black Children, Roots, Culture, and Learning Styles* looks at this same area for African American children in general.

The last area that contributes to the decline of the African American boys' test scores is the lack of male teachers. Up until this point, African American boys probably have not had the opportunity to experience an African American male teacher. I was very fortunate, when I was growing up at a very critical age and in the fourth grade, to have had a Black male teacher by the name of Mr. Payne. Unfortunately, most of our boys will go to kindergarten through the eighth grade without a Black male teacher. I believe that in order to *be* a Black man you need to *see* Black men. I indicated earlier that our present number of Black male teachers, is only 1.2 percent. The overall shortage of Black teachers will become more acute for Black males by the year 2000. Again, I ask the question to the larger community, how are we going to develop Black boys to be men, if they have not seen one? Why do we not want to educate our children?

When America had an extreme shortage of math and science teachers, schools altered their criteria and qualifications and allowed professionals in other fields to teach, such as engineers and accountants. Provisions were made to provide the training, course work, and pedagogy. Many private schools have became very successful with this solution. This adjustment was able to remedy the problem that we had in math and science. I believe the same urgency, if not greater, exists with African American male teachers.

It's obvious that the present power structure does not value this as much as I do, so it is up to the larger African American community to put pressure on school districts to come up with programs and provisions that will increase the number of African American teachers, specifically male.

There is a movement afloat in many states to entice younger students into considering teaching. In Iowa, they are working with sixth through eighth grade students promising scholarships if they agree to teach. I commend these efforts, and we need more incentives such as this.

The long term solution is to have role models inspire our students at a very young age to consider teaching, and especially Black male students. Secondly, we need to have institutions that will provide scholarship monies if they promise to teach. Several private schools have responded to these suggestions. These institutions literally went to the streets, community colleges, and other places and saw potential in Black males and cultivated that potential. Now they are reaping the benefits of having some very positive Black males in their classrooms.

I am very much aware of the problems that may occur from unions who often times want to maintain the status quo, but we need creative administrators who will respond, as Malcolm use to say, "By any means necessary." We need to find ways to increase the number of African American teachers in our classroom. If we cannot increase the number of African American males in a classroom on a full-time basis, then every effort should be made by each school to develop the program, "A Hundred Black Men". I am pleased to see the large number of programs that are in each city. I just do not believe that 100 Black men in Chicago, New York, LA, Washington or Atlanta will arrest the problem that we are currently experiencing. We need them for each school, not just each city.

Two programs I think are doing an excellent job at intervening at the right time with the proper strategy are in Waterloo, Iowa and Houston, Texas. The program in Waterloo is designed to identify 50 to 75 "at risk" Black boys in fourth grade and identify Black male role models who will spend 4 to 6 hours a week interacting with the child. In-service training is also provided for the teacher and parents. I had the fortunate opportunity to speak at a banquet and in a very moving ceremony there were 75 Black men in front of me, and 75 boys in front of them. During the program the men put a piece on kinte cloth around the shoulders of the boys and made a commitment that they would remain in contact with the boys through their 18th birthday.

The program was only funded for 1 to 3 years, and like most governmental programs just when people are beginning to remove the bugs and idiosyncrasies from the operation the monies end. We need to begin to build programs like we built pyramids. Our ancestors built the pyramid of Gizeh 2700 BC which later became one of the seven wonders of the world and the only one still standing. We build pyramids that last over 5000 years, and programs that die in three years.

I was also impressed that the program was in Waterloo not New York, Chicago, or Los Angeles. My only desire is that we need to institute more programs of this caliber. Another program that I respect greatly is the Fifth Ward Enrichment program in Houston. The combination of role models going into the schools, providing counseling and tutoring during the school day and providing recreational and informational sessions in the evenings and on the weekends has been very successful. Most schools do not have counselors at the elementary school level and an inadequate number at the high school level. The ratio of student/counselor borders between three and five hundred to one. It has become obvious that very little counseling is taking place and children that are at risk, specifically Black boys need counseling before high school. We need more adults, specifically African American males that will consider counseling and tutoring our youth.

If we cannot do a better job of developing African American boys to their fullest potential then I recommend an extreme solution and that being, the design of a Black male classroom.

In 1985, I recommended this to a private school in Newark, New Jersey. I also recommended this solution at the 1989 National Association of Black School Education's (NABSE) national conference in Portland, Oregon. I have been interviewed by numerous newspapers and magazines, including Education Week and Time about the needs and components that would make up the Black male classroom. My publishing company, African American Images, has a curriculum division called SETCLAE (Self Esteem Through Culture Leads to Academic Excellence), where consultants are trained to help school districts design and develop these classes.

The major components of the Black male classroom would be as follows:

- Black Male Teachers
- 20-24 Students
- Cooperative Learning
- SETCLAE Curriculum
- Physical Education
- Daily Nutritional Meals
- Science Lab
- Martial Art Training
- Phonics
- Musical Instruments
- Whole-Brain Lesson Plans and Tests
- Math Word Problems
- Junior Business League
- Corporate Sponsors for Summer Employment
- Academic Contests and Assemblies
- Monthly Parent Meetings

The above represents the kind of classes and schools we would like to have for all children, but especially for African American male children. Our staff would train the teachers on expectations, learning styles, SETCLAE, cooperative learning and all the components that would best socialize our boys. This kind of setting would no longer place Black boys in the tenuous position of being compared to female students who have matured faster, and taught exclusively by female teachers.

This classroom will correct the problem of Black boys not having an African American male teacher. This solution would channel the energy that boys have through daily physical education and martial arts. The competence that boys demonstrate with objects and artifacts will be helpful if they are involved in a science lab and a regular science project. The ability boys have in music will be used to show its relationship to mathematics.

This classroom will offer critical thinking skills. The use of word problems and establishing a junior business league, which will try to show the relevance of the classroom to the streets. It should be an amazement to everyone that the same boy that failed math in a classroom is able to measure kilos and grams for drugs and convert it to dollars and cents. The major objection that I've heard is that having an all Black male classroom is discriminatory and it goes back to segregated classrooms. What is puzzling about these comments is that the classroom is already segregated when we have 75 percent or more African American boys in special ed and remedial class. Nobody seems to object to that. My recommendation is that since the boys are already in a separate class, why don't we take advantage of the opportunity, both for the students that are in these classes as well as high achieving male students. I'm glad that there are some creative and committed superintendents and administrators who are now pursuing this particular classroom and how we can avoid the legal implications.

The other comment that I've heard about this recommendation is, how are we going to staff a Black male classroom when there are very few Black male teachers available? Previously, I mentioned several strategies, initiatives, and programs addressing this issue. The proper commitment and advertising, should nullify this concern.

I also recommended at the NABSE convention, a moratorium on special ed placements for the African American male child, except in extreme cases. The numbers have reached a proportion where something is wrong with how we are classifying children. Anytime we see figures where 17 percent of public school children are African American, but 41 percent of the children are placed in special ed and 85 percent of the time they are African American male children, something is wrong with the way the *system* classifies children, and not the *children* themselves.

It is also imperative that we understand that 5 percent of the teachers make 30 percent of the referrals. A better solution, would be mandating in-service training or the removal of the teacher. The problem is, teachers have a union and African American boys do not. I have chosen to become a representative of the Black boys' union. We need more adults to stop this onslaught.

In Detroit, a pilot program has been implemented where rather than removing the child from the mainstream classroom and into special ed, they bring the special ed resources to the children. Many schools have become trigger happy and pull children out to increase funds to their school district. This is not totally their fault. Schools receive additional monies based upon classifying students both at the upper and lower extreme. Consequently, schools receive additional funds for having gifted and talented and special ed students, not students that are in the middle.

I cannot stress enough to parents that one of the most important meetings of your child's life will be the meeting that will determine whether your child will go into special ed. The meeting will consist of a principal, teacher, social worker, and psychologist. In most schools, once the recommendation has been made by the teacher, the social worker, psychologist and principal will concur. This meeting can be very intimidating for a low income single parent when meeting with four educated people who recommended that the child be placed in special ed. My major concern is that the aggregate figures in special ed are the result of each one of these individual meetings. Each of these meetings contribute to the large number of Black boys that may not receive a high school diploma, may not go on to college, may end up in prison, and not become productive husbands and fathers. I just feel that we cannot afford to lose any more boys to special ed.

A study that was reported in October 1987, "Harvard Education and Review", indicated that special ed may not be special. The only thing that may be special is that African American children are placed there *more* than anyone, stay *longer* than anyone else, and don't return back to the main classroom on *grade level*. What makes it special? How do we evaluate special ed?

Again parents, I cannot stress enough that you have to meet teachers where they are. If a lack of understanding exists between the classroom teachers and Black male students, then we must develop programs and literature that help educators understand how children learn or consider placing a moratorium on special ed placement. We must increase the number of Black male teachers or design a Black male classroom; and parents must increase the amount of study and quiet time at home and reduce the amount of time that our children spend watching television, talking on the telephone, listening to the radio or record player and playing Nintendo. During this period of pre-adolescence (9 through 13), we need parents who will have their sons read to them. Parents should not accept their pre-adolescents being illiterate. Unfortunately, many parents are not aware that their thirteen year old son is reading on a primary level.

During this period of pre-adolescence, it has been previously mentioned that peer pressure has now become the greatest influence on many of our children. We will probably never be able to reduce the power of peer pressure but what we can do is infiltrate and incorporate our values into the peer group to reinforce academic achievement. In my earlier book entitled, *To Be Popular or Smart: The Black Peer Group*, I indicated that it has now reached such negative proportions that when our children are doing a good job in school, many of them are teased, especially when a boy is doing well. Now it becomes even harder when they are on the honor roll because they are accused of "acting white" and when they speak proper english they receive the same accusation.

One of the ways we can circumvent this trend is to use the

peer group to reinforce academic achievement. The method that can achieve this is cooperative learning. In a typical classroom of 30 children, teachers normally grade on a curve. Grades are based on the highest score achieved and distribution ranges are determined accordingly. With cooperative learning, children are divided into groups and they receive a team grade and an individual grade. What is ironic is that African American children, especially boys, do everything together, but study. They play ball, listen to records, develop rap songs, get high, and hang out together. It is only in the classroom that they are viewed as individuals. Studies also show that Asian students score higher for several reasons, with one being they study together. Cooperative learning is one way to use the peer group to reinforce academic achievement.

The use of cooperative learning will reduce the teacher having to tell students to be quiet, be still, and return back to the lesson because the group reinforces positive behavior. It is very enjoyable to see students on the same team discipline and motivate each other toward academic excellence.

It is also imperative that schools realize that they are often giving mixed and negative messages to children on what they value. Schools give more glory to their ballplayers than to their scholars. We give medals, trophies, and pep rallies to the basketball and football team and give little certificates, buttons and medals for the debate, spelling bee, and science fair winners.

Schools must show that they value academic achievement more than athletics and they must also reinforce it with the kind of pomp and glorification that is given to sports.

It is during pre-adolescence that many adults have growing concerns about the self-esteem of their children. Many people feel that Black boys suffer from low self-esteem. In the first chapter, we indicated that self-esteem is very complex and that a person may be very confident and have a healthy dose of self-esteem in one endeavor and may be very intimidated and hesitant in another. I take the position that Black boys do not suffer from low self-esteem outside of the classroom, and are very confident with their friends, girl-friends, and other social activities. I

40

believe that schools that have placed Black boys in lower track classes, remedial reading, special ed, labeled them hyperactive and not given them high expectations, contribute to their low self-esteem in the classroom. I also think that it is very significant that African American boys who may have been destroyed in the classroom, have insulated themselves with Black culture in the Black community and have found a way to feel good about themselves irrespective of the schools. Gangs and rap records are expressions of this phenomenon.

The last item that I would like to look at in this chapter is the significance that *sports* has had on the African American male, especially at the impressionable ages of nine through thirteen.

In speaking to students across the country, I often ask the boys to share with me their career goals. More than half the group will tell me that they plan to go to the NBA, NFL or major league baseball. Because I am a strong advocate of developing self-esteem, the last thing that I want to do is to destroy someone's dream of becoming a professional ballplayer. However, I do attempt to make the students aware that the odds are one million to 35 that they will achieve this objective and the odds are better that they will become engineers, computer programmers, or doctors.

The significance of sports has less impact on female students and students involved in sports not traditionally viewed as money makers, ie. track, wrestling, swimming, and gymnastics. I had the fortunate experience of running track in high school and college. It not only financially assisted me through college, it kept me in excellent shape, gave me a positive male role model (my coach), and helped to develop my character. It did not give me the illusion that I did not need to study because I was going to the NBA.

The big three are basketball, football, and baseball, and in that order of popularity. Many high school coaches in football and baseball, tell me that it is even difficult for them to attract athletes because of the tremendous influence that basketball has on our youth. Presently 86 percent of the NBA starters are African American while less than two percent of the doctors, engineers, and dentists are African American.

The National Collegiate Athletic Association (NCAA) propositions 42 and 48 are attempts to re-orientate our students and place the priority on academics. Unfortunately, the pressure is placed exclusively on the athletes and not on the schools and coaches. I commend people like John Thompson at Georgetown, who understood that a Patrick Ewing in four years can bring 12 million dollars to Georgetown via television contracts and it will only cost Georgetown $50,000 in scholarships. This is probably the best return on an investment any business can possibly have. Coaches like John Thompson took the position that as long as Patrick Ewing is going to make that kind of money for the university, let's at least make sure that he graduates, and if it requires a tutor after practice, on the plane and in the hotel it should be allocated, and if necessary, an extension of one year for a five year scholarship. I like the legislation requiring schools to disclose their graduation records on its athletes.

The major point is that our girls do not suffer from the illusion of going to the NBA. Every effort should be made to try to reduce the impact that money making sports have on our youth. I have observed schools where 200 athletes have tried out for ten athletic teams. Basketball, football, baseball, wrestling, swimming, track, gymnastics and the others, and a hundred of the two hundred tried out for the basketball team, 25 for football, 25 for baseball, and the other 50 students tried out for the remaining seven sports. I try to convince youth they have a much better chance making the swimming or track team than making the basketball team. This may be an excellent opportunity to secure a scholarship and develop your career. Youth, especially between the ages of nine and thirteen don't care about odds. They believe that they will be the one out of a hundred on their high school team and one out of a million going to the NBA.

In conclusion, we must again assess how well our boys are doing in the seven areas, or barometers we are trying to use to monitor our boys growth and development: spirituality, racial awareness, scholarship, school, self-esteem, peer pressure, respect for authority, and responsibility. We don't lose our boys instantaneously, we lose them when they are not growing spiritually, when they become cynical and have disdain reading about their history, as their reading level and math scores begin to lag behind the national average. We lose our boys when they begin to lack confidence in school, not wanting to read out loud, going up to the board, answering questions, and not volunteering to be in public programs. We must monitor the influence of the peer group. This is a volatile period when they may become involved with gangs. It is our responsibility to monitor the time and influence that the peer group has on our children.

In *To Be Popular or Smart: The Black Peer Group*, I indicated that good parents *know* their children's friends, *invite* them over, *program* the activities, and make sure they *check* back ever so often. Children that leave home at one o'clock in the afternoon on Saturday should be seen before 10 and 11 o'clock that night. We must monitor whether or not our boys are respecting authority, from the home and all other adults.

Finally, in the pre-adolescent period between 9 and 13 our boys should become more responsible. In the areas of personal hygiene, their choice of clothes, cleaning their rooms, care for siblings, money management, and their studies.

In the next chapter we will look at the adolescent age range between 13 and 18. This is where society becomes fully aware of all the problem areas we neglected for the first 13 years.

Adolescence will reflect how well we've done our job.

Chapter 3

Adolescence (13 through 18)

"I don't even recognize my son, does he love me? I think he shows me. I'm not going to ever have children again, something happens to them when they become 13. They must all take some pill or drug or go to another planet called teenageville. When he was in 2nd grade he use to run home from school and tell me about his spelling grades. I used to love it when he called me mama. He could always get what ever he wanted from me when he said, 'Mama, I love you'. But last night, I asked him where was he going and when he would be coming back. He looked at me, then he looked through me and for a moment, I was afraid of him. It was as if my 17 year old son had never come out of me".

These are just some of the comments from parents, especially mothers who are wondering and grappling with how they can go through this next hurdle. Adolescence is a very trying period, especially for sons and their mothers. It's also a challenging time for larger communities. This age group of males literally controls the community; has it in a state of fear where women, elders, and often times, men do not want to walk the streets at night because of these male predators, ages 13 to 18. They appear to be angry. This age group has forced schools to consider whether or not they should have guards at every door or metal detectors. Teachers are now more concerned about safety than education, and students are often afraid to walk to school.

Let's return back to the mother and son relationship. Many parents want a buddy-to-buddy relationship with their children, to be on a first name basis. I talk to boys who see their mother as their girlfriend or some girl to have a conversation. Many boys feel that their mother is always nagging them about doing their chores, their homework, and other responsibilities. Boys have often told me that they have eight times to empty the garbage when their mother tells them to do it, because the first seven times the mother is nagging them and on the eighth time she becomes very assertive and gives a very clear message on what she wants done, and the boys understand it.

In *Countering the Conspiracy to Destroy Black Boys Vol II*, I wrote about the concept of some mothers who *raise* their daughters and *love* their sons. They teach their daughters to study, cook, sew, attend church, and expose them to various other educational and cultural programs and leave it optional for their sons. One of the major difficulties that youth workers mentioned, is the lack of support they receive from parents with this age group. The two earlier age groups, infancy through nine and 9 through 13; at this stage parents were more supportive at mandating their children's attendance in constructive programs. For some reason, parents who are now buddies with their sons allow them to decide whether they should go to church, attend an extra tutorial session and become involved in extra-curricular activities.

I suggested in the book, *To Be Popular of Smart: The Black Peer Group*, the need for parents to organize a parental support group so that the mothers can openly discuss teenage children, primarily their boys. Many parents are responding to these situations individually and feel isolated from the larger community. Often, the problem may not be resolved in the support group, but the very fact of knowing you're not the only one experiencing this situation is consoling. I'm optimistic that not only can we provide a bond for each other, but I believe that solutions can come out of these sessions.

This period of adolescence, ages 13 through 18, is when the larger society begins to acknowledge the male shortage. It has even been brought to my attention by high school staff, that the junior and senior prom is not always attended by both males and females. That large numbers of females go unescorted to the prom. When I first heard this, it was mind boggling. I just couldn't comprehend that girls would go to the prom without a date. The staff went on to tell me that the girls chose to attend; that the alternative was to refrain from attending a very memorable experience in their lives. I was aware that girls don't often go to the prom with someone in their class, but not being able to find a male in their immediate vicinity illustrates the magnitude of this problem.

When you observe the freshman class, you still see numbers that are relatively equal; a small shortage may exist. In typical classes of 600 freshman, there will be 325 girls and 275 boys. Four years later approximately 300 students will graduate. Two hundred of those students will be female and at most a hundred of the students will be male. In such a short period of time, we lost 175 to 200 students. Although this book is being written about Black male development, we are also concerned about the 125 female students that we also lost for a myriad of reasons, with one of the major factors being teenage pregnancy.

There are numerous issues that contribute to the high male dropout rate in this country. In large urban areas, the dropout rate hovers near 50 percent and in a few cities the percentage is greater than 50 percent. The factors include our children being bored, lack of finances, lack of rewarding experiences in school, lack of positive adult reinforcement, and concern for gangs and safety. Our boys are extremely bored with an irrelevant curriculum presented with low teacher's expectations.

Schools are giving children a 1910 curriculum in the 1990s. I had the experience when speaking to a particular group of teachers in New York, to have them tell me that Black boys were not good in math. One of them admitted that they did an excellent job on the metric part of the curriculum, and she wondered why. Then several people started smiling because when Black boys heard terms like kilos and grams, their interest perked because they finally saw relevance between the classroom and the streets.

I enjoy speaking to all groups, students, parents, and teachers, but the group that gives me the greatest satisfaction is adolescent boys. Schools often tell me they are undisciplined, disrespectful, and have short attention spans. Educators are amazed to see their boys respond so well. I tell them my success at bonding with these students is due to my relationship with God; I told them the truth, and they knew it came from their brother who loves them. What I like about our youth is that they're honest. They tell you exactly how they feel. When they hear the truth from someone who cares about them, they will be disciplined and respectful.

We have to improve our curriculum by making it multi-cultural, Africentric, and relevant. It is rewarding how a simple change in the curriculum could reduce the dropout rate and improve attendance. You can not separate curriculum from the disseminator; they are part of the same package. I believe that there are three kinds of adults in our classrooms, instructors, teachers, and coaches. Instructors specialize in dispensing information. Many of them will tell you they teach geometry, physics or english. Instructors don't teach *children*, they teach their *subjects*. Instructors are people that desire to be college professors. Teachers, on the otherhand, not only understand their subject matter, but also understand learning styles. Coaches have the ability to combine subject matter and learning styles with identity and self-esteem.

Unfortunately from the fourth grade on we have an increasing number of instructors teaching our youth. Most African American boys require coaches that understand content, learning styles, and self-esteem. We need *coaches* not *instructors* to teach our students.

It has been rewarding visiting high schools where many of my friends are coaches, they almost single-handedly decreased the dropout rate, because of the bond that they shared with the students. The students do not want to disappoint the coach. One committed coach in the lives of our children can make the difference.

My concern lies in that coaches burn out faster than instructors. Coaches give more and are the minority. Instructors, who are the majority give less, are often found in the teacher's lounge condeming our youth seldom burn out. We need strong administrators who will find creative ways to keep our coaches inspired and hold instructors accountable.

The high dropout rate is also a result of the disproportionate number of Black males suspended. African American males are eight percent of public school students nationwide, but constitute 37 percent of the suspensions. Numerous studies indicate they are suspended for infractions while other students receive warnings, for the same violation. African American males that have been suspended for an abundant number of days risk the possibility of matriculation based on attendance requirements.

My travels have taken me to school districts where a major difference exists in the suspension rates at high schools who have similar demographics. Why is it that one high school with an effective administrator, a committed staff, and clearly stated guidelines can possess a much lower suspension rate than another school? We can't afford to lose African American boys to ineffective schools nor have them fail due to suspension. For these reasons, I'm also in favor of in-house suspension. In this way, the violation will be served, but attendance will be maintained. My staff at African American Images has designed the Malcolm X room, to provide an educational and cultural experience for the infraction. We will train the designated staff and provide resource materials for its successful operation. The staff member would provide the youth with a program similar to "Scared Straight". It would be mandatory that everyone would read the "Autobiography of Malcolm X". My only hesitancy is that more students may choose to be suspended to take advantage of this cultural experience. If that happens, hopefully it would inspire administrators to make their curriculum more multicultural and Africentric.

I feel high schools are too large, and not designed to produce critically thinking youth. These schools offer an economy of scales, whereby you can offer a hundred and fifty different courses under one roof. In order to offer such a wide variety of courses you will need a large student body. It has become obvious to me that our youth may look older, but they are still immature and very impressionable. Schools with two to five thousand students, who are exposed to drugs, sexual promiscuity, and venereal diseases, may be too much for them (a limited staff) to handle. It is for this reason that with my younger son, I chose to place him in a high school with a small student body, where all the teachers would know him and give the proper direction.

I also find it ironic that the inmate to guard ratio is far smaller than the student/teacher ratio and definitely smaller than the student/counselor ratio. Our government will spend 18 to 38 thousand dollars to incarcerate someone and will not spend additional money for teachers and counselors. I postulate that an increase in counselors will reduce the prison population. Can you imagine a large group of African American males committing themselves to going to the schools once a month as counselors. These men would listen and discuss with the students their goals, plans, and aspirations. I mentioned earlier, another major reason for the high dropout rate is finances and gangs. I believe succinctly that the struggle is parents, teachers, and concerned community citizens against dealers, gangs, and the media for the minds of our children.

Let's review the messages that each group gives to our children.

Gangs, Dealers, and Media	Parents, Teachers, and Concerned Community Citizens
2 to 8 hours spent together. As age increases, involvement increases.	7 to 34 minutes spent together. As age increases involvement decreases.
They listen *to* each other.	They talk *at* each other.
Immediate gratification	Long-term gratification
Materialism, designer clothing, bright colors (large/flashy)	Internal, moral, integrity, honesty
Advocate money via drugs, sports, music, crime, and lottery	Money via good education and working hard.

It should become obvious to the reader that we are not going to win against gangs, dealers, and the media with fathers and mothers spending 7 and 34 minutes respectively, and instructors spending 40 to 45 minutes disseminating irrelevant information to their youth. Many youth tell me that adults in the neighborhood don't even say hello. Many adults in the neighborhood tell me they're afraid of our youth. Isn't it interesting that as our youth become older, they spend more time together, while most adults involvement is on the decline.

If you gave most adults an opportunity to make hundreds and thousands of dollars a day versus years of service, many adults would also choose the former. In one of my earlier books, titled *Motivating and Preparing Black Youth To Work*, I mentioned that for many of us life has been reduced to money. Our youth via gangs, dealers, and media have found five other ways to make money beside a good education and working hard. Our competition now has become drugs, sports, music, crime, and the lottery. It becomes very hard competing against those areas. However, I do feel that as adults, we can still show there are still better odds via a good education than the million to one odds of going to the NBA and the chance of selling drugs for forty years, retiring, and living off a pension. Ultimately, I think that we have to show youth that life is about more than money. It's about finding something that you enjoy so much that you are willing to do it for free, but because you do it so well, you get paid for it. It becomes imperative that adults help young people to identify and develop their talents and show them related careers. The above chart was offered in an attempt for us to become crystal clear on our competition. Like a chess or basketball game, we need to design and carve out a strategy that will reclaim our youth.

At this critical period of adolescence, the media has an onslaught on our youth. Advertisers have found this a major market and that youth often influence their parents purchasing habits. The African American community is only 12 percent of the nation's population, but we consume 38 percent of the liquor and 39 percent of the cigarettes. Health director Sullivan, Reverend Butts, Father Clements, Father Pfleger, and many others need to be commended for the strong stand they have taken on trying to reduce the consumption of nicotine, alcohol, and harder drugs.

Sullivan publicly stated to the tobacco industry that it is unethical to directly market cigarettes to Black males. Reverend Butts of Abyssinia Church in New York, and the larger community has put a great degree of pressure on billboard advertising companies to either remove the billboards or they would deface them. Father Clements and Pfleger, Dick Gregory and others organized, to make sure stores did not sell drug paraphernalia.

I recommend that educators, concerned community citizens, and parents cut out advertisements in magazines, cover up the company name and ask the youth what's being advertised? Often times in my youth sessions, I will display ads that are supposedly advertising liquor, cigarettes, and cosmetics but in actuality, they are subconsciously advertising a good time, sexual activity, and materialism. The illusion is that smoking and drinking will improve your looks, provide a fancy car, and people of the opposite sex will be attracted to you.

Many of our youths' first encounter with smoking, drinking, and sexual activity is during adolescence. A decision to start smoking at 14 may very well determine premature death at 34. A decision to become sexually active at 14 may determine a family on welfare for the rest of their lives. Some youth lack education about their bodies, birth control, and pregnancy. I have heard horror stories where youth did not think that they could get pregnant during the first six months of sexual activity. Some youth who had become pregnant thought, just like with other problems, time would remove it and chose not tell their parents. This miseducation will continue as long as the peer group spends more time with our children than we do. It really does takes a whole village to raise a child.

At the beginning of this chapter, we mentioned that this age group of Black males has the larger community held hostage. Elders, children, women, and some men are afraid to walk the streets at night. We also mentioned that this is another reason for a high dropout rate. Some schools are simply not safe, inside or outside.

There is a need for adults to show African American males in this age group a way to resolve their problems through non-violence. My staff at African American Images has also designed a program called The Dr. King Nonviolence Laboratory. This experience was established primarily for junior and senior high schools. They would teach designated staff and or students how to resolve conflict through nonviolence. Dr. King's theory does not need to be buried between 1929 and 1968. We need to show African American males how they can preserve their manhood without having to kill someone because they step on their shoe, brush up against them, possess a pair of designer shoes or starter jacket that they envy or what ever else seems to irritate

African American males.

The term Black on Black crime is often used by the media. We never hear the term White on White crime. Any criminologist will tell you that crime usually takes place between people that are related, know each other or live in the same proximity. Homicide is the leading killer for this age group; it becomes essential that we teach African American males how to resolve conflict via non-violence. There is a program in Chicago, within a high school, where a hundred Black men volunteer on a regular basis to teach Black boys a strategy of non-violence and conflict management.

Our laboratory includes role-playing, where two African American males brush up against one another, express themselves the way they would normally on the streets. Of course, in this role-playing we are not going to allow them to hit each other, but all body language, hostility and all other expressions are released. We then bring them together as if it was the beginning of a boxing match. We have them look at each other, and in front of the group reveal the reason why they hate their *brother*, is because they hate *themselves*. We will expose them to Dr. King and his theories of nonviolence. Groups can also consider, if they must, allowing boys to resolve conflict through public competition; Indian wrestling, pushups, or bench pressing.

In *Countering the Conspiracy to Destroy Black Boys* Volume II, I mentioned the concept of a "battle" and "war." Some Black boys think that talking back to their mothers, female teachers, and the police, is a form of manhood. We need programs and men that will teach Black boys the distinction between a battle and a war and that it may be better to keep your mouth shut and lose the battle to be available for the war in the liberation of our people. The police often know how to bait Black boys into making a mistake. Too many African American males made a wise crack or a wrong move and were shot by the police. Churches, schools, and community groups need to establish a better relationship with the police so that we can reclaim our youth. Our males are being seized by the gangs, dealers, the media, police, and the penal institutions.

54

A professional organization called Noble (National Organization of Black Law Enforcement) is an attempt to organize African American superintendents, captains, and other high ranking officials to begin viewing law enforcement from the vantage point of prevention, rather than responding to a crisis. The relationship with the police department and African American community will not be effective in the heat of a crisis when another Black male has been shot in the back. It needs to be developed by an ongoing watchdog committee and NOBLE representatives. Efforts should be made, inspite of the backlash to affirmative action to increase the percent of African American police officers commensurate with the percent of African American people in the city. There are numerous cities where the African American population is fifty percent or better and the African American police officers constitute less than 20 percent of the staff and a smaller percentage of the officers. This inequity is further exasperated in prisons spread across the state, in rural areas miles from the African American community.

A good friend of mine, a respected judge, Eugene Pincham has brought a great degree of sensitivity to his court. He has done research pointing out that 95 percent of the people that went through his court did not possess a high school diploma nor did they attend Sunday School. He and others have designed programs like "Probate Challenge" which allows youth on probation to be given academic assistance, role-models, and cultural awareness. It provides a positive transition from probation to the real world. We need more programs like this when 25 percent of our male population is involved with the penal institutions and 47 percent of all inmates are African American.

It is much that we can do for our boys. Many are angry. Here is an example of a boy that is on the streets and could kill you due to lack of nurturance. Darryl is 16 years of age, it's 5 o'clock in the afternoon; he's been outside on the streets since 11 o'clock that morning. There were a couple of times when he could have gotten high; he passed it up. There were a couple of opportunities, to rob from a store, and steal a car. He robbed the store, but chose not to steal a car. There was a chance to meet three females over someone's house where the parents were not there. He said he may check it out later that evening, and that he was going home to get something to eat.

He walked into the house and his mother (who was not home when he left at 11 o'clock) sort of looked at him and shook her head, while she continued to talk with her friend on the telephone. Darryl goes into the kitchen where there is nothing to eat. The mother then yells, "Why did you come back in here anyway; get your head out of that refrigerator...sometimes I wish you were never born". Darryl stomps outside.

This is one example of the kind of male child on our streets. One who is angry, suffering from a lack of nurturance and acceptance, and hungry for love. He gravitates toward his peers, gangs, young ladies that give him a two minute thrill, and drugs that may give him a short-term high.

In the White community, they too have wayward boys. Boys that don't always do their homework, who don't always come home on time, and who are often involved with crime. In the typical White community, 16 year old Joey has been acting up in the neighborhood, thrown a couple of balls in neighbors' windows, and caused a minor disturbance in front of a cleaners and grocery store. One evening four or five White male adults, three of them business owners, and two concerned citizens decide to talk with Joey while he's idling away on the street. They tell him in no uncertain terms that they are not going to allow that; "We are going to give you a job at the cleaners, and if you do well, we will find you another job at the plant or come up with some money to send you to college".

I call this the "safety net". When the home and school fails, children need a community safety net. In most communities safety nets are spearheaded by the business sector. The business sector not only has the financial resources to respond, but the commitment to its youth and desire to make sure their communities are safe for business growth and expansion is enormous. In the African American community when the home and school breaks down, the lack of the safety net by the church and the business sector has accelerated the number of African

American male youth that have become a threat to the people they encounter. I often tell people while my father was my best role model, it was my track coach who created a safety net that prevented me from spending idle time on the streets.

We need businesses, churches, community organizations, and concerned African American men to identify adolescent male youth and provide them with a safety net which includes direction, high expectations, employment opportunities,and educational advancement. This may be one of the weakest factors in our communities, that our safety net is not strong due to the lack of business development and lack of overall compassion to respond to youth that are not biologically ours, but who belong to the African village. It should be obvious that a single parent and two parents are not going to be as successful as a village raising children.

The struggle has come down to adults against gangs for the minds of our children, and "Rites of Passage" organizations against gangs for the minds of our children. Jeff Fort, a major gang leader of the "Chicago Blackstone Rangers" once told me, "We will always have the youth because we make them feel important". I'll never forget that; Fort is a gangbanger who understood psychology very well. One of the major ways of attracting people to your organization is spending time with them and making them feel important. In that respect, the gangs do a very good job. It is now the responsibility of the adult community to also give our youth some of our time to make them feel important.

Fathers are not going to win the battle for our youth spending only seven minutes a day with their sons. Men are not going to capture the imagination of male youth when the Cub and Boy Scouts in many areas are now being administered by women. I don't believe that African American women want these positions, but they do want their sons in constructive activities. If men are not going to respond, then by default women will fill the void.

Our boys desperately want to know what it means to be a man. In this society manhood is based more from a physical perspective, machoism, how much reefer you can smoke, wine you can drink, how many women you have, how many babies you make, how well you can fight, how many people you've killed and how many times you can go to jail and come out unrehabilitated.

In a book by Ray Raphael, *The Men From The Boys*, he describes what it's like when urban male youth do not receive a clear definition of manhood:

Traditional cultures throughout the world have often devised ways of dramatizing and ritualising the passage into manhood and of transforming that passage into a community event. Through the use of structured initiation rites, these societies have been able to help and guide the youths through their period of developmental crisis. By formalizing the transitional process, complex problems of identity formation are translated into concrete and straightforward tasks. Often, the trials a youth must endure are extreme:

Throughout their journey, the elders belaboured them with firebrands, sticks tipped with obsidian and nettles. They arrived covered with blood and were received by a pair of guardians. A period of seclusion followed, during which the boys had to undergo a series of trials. They were beaten, starved, deprived of sleep, partially suffocated, and almost roasted. Water was forbidden, and if thirsty they had to chew sugar-cane. Only the coarsest foods were allowed, and even these were left raw. All the time the guardians gave them instructions about kinship, responsibilities, and duties to their seniors. At length, after some months, the priest summoned the supernatural monsters from underground while the other men sounded the bull-roarers. The guardians now taught their charges how to incise the penis in order to eliminate the contamination resulting from association with the other sex. Subsequently, this operation had to be performed regularly. A series of great feasts then took place, and initiands emerged richly decorated.

This is how a Busama youth in the highlands of New Guinea proves his manhood. As odd as the rituals might sound to us, their impact is forceful and direct: If a youth can make it through this bizarre sequence of mutilation and deprivation, then certainly he can handle the everyday hardships he will confront throughout his adult life. Dramatically and emphatically, he has repudiated the vulnerability of boyhood while asserting the toughness and resilience required of in manhood. In his own eyes and in the eyes of society, he has shown himself to be worthy of adult respect.

Perhaps we have something to learn from this primitive Rites of Passage. The underlying structure of the ritual is enviable, even if the details might seem sordid. Listen, for example, to a typical reaction of a modern day man to the crude but gutsy Busama initiation rituals:

I wish I had it that easy. Run through the fire, step on the coals—then it's over and done with. You're a man, everyone knows you're man, and that's the end of it. For me it keeps on going on and on. The uncertainty of it-at any moment you could be out on the streets. It's all tied up with money. I've got to keep on fighting for money and respect. The fire never stops; I keep running through it every day.(Howard R.)[1]

I have been actively involved over the years in assisting "Rites of Passage" organizations. We need them in every city, neighborhood, and literally every block. In the previous Volumes of this book, we talked about how to form these programs. The books included how to organize the adult male population, the need for study and bonding among this group, identifying a facility, recruitment strategy, desired age range, and the number of youth you wish to serve.

This book will look at the minimal standards that most

"Rites of Passage" organizations have agreed to adhere to, but more importantly, examples of lesson plans to be used to reinforce these minimal standards. The minimal standards include: African and African American history, economics, politics, family responsibility, career development, spirituality, community involvement and organizing, physical fitness, and the Nguzo Saba value system, all taught from an Africentric perspective.

The objective is to have the youth master a predetermined criteria in these respected areas. Lesson plans are then designed to assist youth in this endeavor. Every effort should be made for the learning experience to be a whole brain approach versus a left-brain approach. There is a strong tendency for African American men to do the exact same thing that teachers do in the classroom, which is to lecture the children or to pass out a ditto sheet. The use of right-brain activities, taking advantage of their interest in music, fine arts, and the use of their hands should be considered. I strongly suggest the usage of our SETCLAE curriculum. The SETCLAE curriculum encompasses all of the above areas. There is no need for each group to have to develop their own individual lesson plans when this curriculum exists and is more than adequate. Listed below are a few suggestions for each category:

African and African-American History
- The development of a family tree.
- Designing a time line from four million years B.C. through 2000 A.D. and placing indicators on the time line of special events that took place in the African experience.
- Reading Lessons from History: *A Celebration In Blackness, The Autobiography of Malcolm X, Manchild In the Promised Land, Native Son, Kaffir Boy,* and *Abdul and the Designer Tennis Shoes.*
- The usage of raps, plays, and debates, incorporating African and African American leaders into the materials.

Economics

- Developing a family budget.
- The ability to read the stock pages.
- Creating an example where a stock/mutual fund was purchased and monitoring over a certain period of time.
- Observing, analyzing, and writing about the types of businesses and business activity in the African American communities.
- Making a product or providing a service and selling it to the larger community, i.e., T-shirts, sweatshirts and memorabilia.
- The development of a business plan.

Politics

- A chart should be designed encompassing local representatives through the presidency and names provided for each and their duties.
- Create a mock election, campaign speeches, and debates.
- Arrange field trips to city, state, national, and international offices. . .i.e., United Nations.
- Being involved in voter registration drives.

Family Responsibilities

- Requiring that the parents design a list of chores and sign the sheet, confirming that the boy has completed these responsibilities.
- Classes in sex education and the distinction between making a baby and taking care of a baby.
- Provide opportunities where boys are involved in cooking, ironing, sewing, and washing dishes. This can be done in an in-house session or at a camp site.

61

- Creating an opportunity for boys to babysit infants and toddlers.
- Teaching the boys carpentry and plumbing.

Career Development
- Have the youth to provide five occupations for each letter of the alphabet.
- Invite guest speakers to talk about their careers.
- Provide tutorial services and awards ceremonies glorifying academic achievement.
- Reviewing course schedules to ensure that career goals can be met.

Spirituality
- Teaching the boys the three components of prayer.
  1. Thanksgiving
  2. Forgiveness of Sin
  3. Request
- Providing the opportunity for boys to pray.
- Reviewing scriptures and placing them into memory.

Community Involvement
- Having the boys to participate in community activities, cleanup drives, walk-a-thons, etc.
- Requiring a minimal number of hours to be volunteered in community organizations.
- Spending time with the homeless and food distribution centers.

Physical Development
- Should include the basic tenets of physical development, sit-ups, push-ups, and running.
- Creating sports contest and junior olympics, martial arts training, drill performances (similar to the Nation of Islam, and fraternities) and teaching health and nutrition.

Nguzo Saba

- UMOJA-unity; teaching the principle of operational unity. There may be 10 items we may be discussing, we disagree on 9. In the spirit of operational unity we will work with the one area we agree.
- KUJICHAGULIA-self determination; not allowing the use of the word can't.
- UJIMA-collective work and responsibility. In all of our programs no one will be allowed to leave, until all of us are finished with the activity.
- UJAMAA-cooperative economic; every effort should be made to pool all resources together and the purchasing of items.
- NIA-purpose; Every member of the Rites of Passage has to declare a career goal and a plan of action on achieving it.
- KUUMBA-the design of tee-shirts, jackets, caps in a very creative fashion
- IMANI-faith; Believing in God, demonstrated by prayers and scripture.

The word "Rites" is plural, meaning there are several stages of mastery. We advocate that the men design a structure allowing boys to matriculate through the stages of Rites of Passage process very similar to the scouts, which had its origins in Africa.

In the African tradition, the Rites of Passage process started with the naming ceremony and ended with becoming an ancestor. The general stages include the naming ceremony, the transition from boyhood to manhood, becoming an adult, and elder. This safeguard is important and will prevent a 14-year-old male who has satisfied the criteria for the Rites of Passage to leave the program or remain and have nothing else to achieve.

Because we are at work against the gangs for the minds of our youth, we must understand the significance of symbols. Our children value T-shirts, sweatshirts, jackets, and caps.

"Rites of Passage" organizations can provide these items with Africentric symbols to reinforce our culture and to create group solidarity.

There have been numerous success stories from "Rites of Passage" organizations nationwide. Some of the major pitfalls are men not remaining consistent with their interaction with the boys, parents who use the programs without giving support back to the organization, and the fact that most "Rites of Passage" organizations are in the larger community and gangs operate on every block. In the African community, all youth went through the same Rites of Passage. Consequently, all youth respected the process. In America, some youth have the fortunate opportunity to experience an Africentric Rites of Passage. However, when returning to their block, the boys may encounter gang members that do not acknowledge the experience, may resent it, and eventually retaliate against the youth. This does not negate the need for the Rites of Passage program; it simply reinforces the need for male consistency, parental involvement, and more Rites of Passage programs that will saturate the community.

As we move into the last chapter, we must again evaluate African Americans with our barometer.

1. Have our boys placed God first in their lives and allowed their decisions to be influenced by this relationship?

2. How do our boys feel about their race of people? Do they look at each other as their brothers and would not do any harm?

3. How are our boys doing in reading and math achievement tests?

4. Do our boys feel good about the school experience? What is their rate of attendance and participating in extra-curriculum activities?

5. How much time do our boys spend with their friends?How late are our boys allowed to stay out? Who is the major influence on their decisions?

6. Do our boys respect their parents, teachers, and elders?
7. Are our boys responsible for their allowance, studies, and their time?

In the final chapter, we will look at the age group that has become a battle cry of the larger African American community. What can we do to save our males between the ages of 18 and 25?

The growth in the economy is white collar jobs, but most African-American males have blue collar skills.

Chapter 4

Adulthood (Ages 18 to 25)

This period in the life of African American males should be the prime of their lives, when they're young, energetic, and strong. It's a time when most young men are moving into the areas of exciting careers, starting their own business, marrying, and starting a family. Unfortunately for African American males, almost every negative statistic is used to describe this period. Homicide, suicide, drug usage, mental insanity, poor health care, unemployment, poverty, educational attainment, crime, and being involved in a penal institution are all factors that are used to describe what should be the zenith of the Black male experience.

It becomes very frustrating for me to travel from city to city and encounter White males who are fresh out of college and the day before were involved in frat bashing and beer fights, and now earn $30,000 plus as sales representatives. This is a very popular position for assertive, aggressive males who did not perform academically in college. They are members of the buddy/buddy club with unlimited income. I really don't see a great difference between a 21 year old White male and an African American male except privilege and a safety net. A safety net that allows White males to matriculate into the larger economy and forces African American males to choose between the military, McDonalds, drugs, and crime. For many African American males, that's how they see their options. If African American men can sell drugs, they can sell Fortune 500 products if given the opportunity. When I speak at schools across the country, I often ask high school seniors what are their plans in September; in many schools, over half of the male population state that they are going to the military. I know that they don't have a burning desire to defend the red, white, and blue in Panama, Jamaica, and Liberia. I do respect these brothers, because they have made their assessment from the options that are available to them, and the military seemed to be the best. If you read studies coming out of various journals and newspapers, it also appears that the military provides a better opportunity for African Americans to advance than the Fortune 500. While that may be true, I remain concerned about African Americans who make up 12 percent of the total U.S. population, but constitute one-third of the military and 41 percent of the Vietnamese causualties.[1] I think that the attraction to the military is more a result of the limited opportunities African Americans feel they have, and the tremendous advertisement campaign of "Be All You Can Be."

This period causes tremendous anguish for African American females, both college graduates and high school dropouts. We have an excess of over 210,000 African American females in college over African American males.[2] When African American females look at figures such as 70 percent of all African American males will be unavailable to them by the year 2000, and some African American females will only consider a male with a college degree who makes over $25,000, they become very discouraged. For females who were not fortunate enough to attend college, who became pregnant, are without a high school diploma and now has more than one child, not only does this group lead in poverty representation, but they also have a very small chance of attracting a husband.

How is a male going to take care of his family when he was born on cocaine, grew up in a household where there was very little quiet time, placed in the lowest reading group and/or special ed, suspended, became a member of a gang, sold drugs, did not meet his first male teacher (other than in physical education) until his junior year of high school,(the year he dropped out), grew up in a low income neighborhood where most adult

African American men are on corners, and by his twenty-first birthday had never seen or heard from his father? Many of our boys experience some of the above and unfortunately, some of our males have experienced all of it. The million dollar question that every group, conference, and concerned committee asks is, "How are we going to reach this group?" It often amazes me that people who raise this question discuss it in the Hyatt Regency, Marriott, and the Hilton while the people they're discussing, have very little opportunity to pay the registration fees or to be comfortable sharing in this kind of setting. I often wonder, do they really want to reach this group? It appears to me that most people are comfortable talking with people that have similar experiences. Some vegetarians don't often feel comfortable around people that eat chitterlings. Some Christians are not comfortable being around Muslims and viceversa. Some people that live in the suburbs and are middle income aren't comfortable around people who live in the city and may be lower income. Do we honestly think that having a conference about the plight of Black males could be resolved at a downtown hotel? Do we leave these conferences with a plan of action that will take us to their community? Do we really love the very brothers that we talk about?

I will never forget a National Urban League Conference held in Atlanta; a street brother found out about the program and came over to the hotel and asked could he earn his registration fee by doing some work because he wanted to participate. It just blew the minds of most of the participants that were there.

In order to save this group, 18 to 25 years old, we are going to have to devise a marketing outreach strategy. A design that was similar to that of Marcus Garvey, the Nation of Islam, Jehovah Witnesses, and progressive Christian churches practicing liberation theology. We will not save this group with institutions that believe they have the answers, but we are going to have to go *inside* the church to receive them. I am so glad that Elijah Muhammad did not wait for Detroit Red to be released from prison to find him.

In my review of teenage pregnancy programs nationwide,

ninety percent of all teenage pregnancy programs counsel the female. We must not believe that men are not responsible, or feel that this group is too difficult to work with, or it's too burdensome to organize them. I reiterate, I think the first step in solving the problem for this age group is that we have to ask ourselves, "Do we really want to interact with this group directly?" If the answer is yes, then the second step is that we have to quit having conferences at downtown hotels and have the programs in the community where these brothers reside.

Also, we have to quit designing these teenage pregnancy programs around the table with coffee and donuts. I propose a better way to attract males would be with male counselors. A man who while playing basketball with the male clients, discuss the same issues without coffee and donuts. The basketball court can be substituted with a weightroom, vocational training room or a pooltable, all items that many female socialworkers wouldn't even consider.

As much as I dislike Jehovah Witnesses knocking on my door, I respect them for believing in their position and willing to take it too the streets. This is what we are going to have to do if we're going to save our males in the prime of their lives.

After we have resolved the major hurdle, the will and the commitment to want to interact with them directly, we must then provide them with shock treatment. We must negate 18 or more years of miseducation.

This shock treatment would include taking them to a prison, and letting them talk to hardcore, but now conscious inmates. We would take them to a drug abuse program and let them witness how difficult it is to withdraw. It would include a trip to a public hospital on a Saturday at midnight to view the tremendous volume of emergencies and then to the morgue. It would incorporate a movie on what crack does to the brain. We would create a dialogue between them and males who thought that they were going to the NBA and musical stardom, only to find out that there is an artificial ceiling created by white power brokers. We would expose them to cultural videos and collectively read and discuss the "Autobiography of Malcolm X". The program would provide them positive male role models, who also had to overcome similar hurdles.

I am not naive. I am very much aware that for some brothers these experiences will not be shock treatment, but will be business as usual. This is why my research has tried to concentrate on intervening at earlier ages. It is more difficult to shock someone who has experienced 18 or more years of a negative lifestyle. For many of our brothers who are moving so fast like Detroit Red, only prison provides the opportunity to fully ascertain their predicament. We have a very "captive audience" of over 609,000 African American males waiting for dedicated teachers who can provide shock treatment.

The African American community cannot afford to lose this many men, while America builds a billion dollar prison industry with poor white workers in rural America. A business that only rehabilitates fifteen percent and has an eighty-five percent recidivism rate. We need a major organization to negotiate with wardens and have conferences at prison sites. Minister Farrakhan from the Nation of Islam has already expressed that he wants them released and taken to an independent land site. What are other leaders saying?

Returning back to my original statement of these activities being shock treatment, unfortunately for some of our males in this age group this will not be shock treatment. Some have experienced greater atrocities and horrifying experiences. However, there are a percentage of males who will be affected by this approach and for that reason it needs to be implemented. For those that are not, we will unfortunately see them in prisons and hopefully not the morgue. As long as they are *alive*, we have an opportunity to *rehabilitate*.

The second step after shock treatment I label, Kunjufu's Wholistic Approach which includes spirituality, African and African-American history, understanding racism, time-management, talent identification and development, proper diet and nutrition, understanding economics, becoming a member of a positive peer group and joining an organization. Lets review these areas in some detail.

I believe that any one of these areas can develop our males to reach their full potential. The more factors working congruently, the more effective the process. When I provide consultations to social service agencies, I recommend that the staff determine which members will be responsible for each area. Any client participating in the program will have to interact with each staff member. The staff will expose the participant to the necessary information in all areas.

Spirituality

One of the major reasons for the rehabilitation of Malcolm X was his coming to grips with his relationship with God. I am a Christian and I am very proud of my relationship with my Lord and Savior, Jesus Christ. This book is not being used as a vehicle to argue about God as much as it is a desire for males to submit themselves to God. I have read numerous articles on this topic; submission in any form, is difficult for males. I believe that this is also the major reason for males having a much higher suicide rate than females—the lack of desire to submit and share their problems with God. In this area, males should be taught the necessity of submission and then learning how to pray and read scriptures.

African and African American History

I posit that one of the major reasons for the success of the Nation of Islam and most Christian churches that have been able to attract men, is they have provided the group with an opportunity to learn and appreciate their culture. For many men they have been taught very little about their history. They, like our people have been given a history where the first day we were in Africa, the second day on the boat and the remaining part of the course was slavery in America. I advocate that if African American men were able to internalize the personalities of Imhotep, King Ramses, King Akhenaten, Toussaint L'ouverture, Nat Turner, Marcus Garvey, Dr. King, and Malcolm X, we would experience self love and self hatred, and homicide would decline.

Racism

Many of our males have not been taught that racism is a sign of insecurity, not inferiority. People that are secure are comfortable with differences. Only insecure people have to rationalize that because they are different, it makes them better. If African people were inferior than there would be no need for discrimination. I argue that racists know more about African Americans than we know about ourselves. In this section, we would explain to the men how special they are and how afraid this country is of African American males reaching their full potential; this explains lynching and castration.

Time Management

Time is the most important resource. It is more valuable than cars, clothes, money, and a mansion. Yet, many African American males in this age group waste their most valuable resource standing on the corner. They have allowed this country to reduce them to a dollar bill. If the country no longer employs them, they hang on the corner and sulk. In this area, we would establish the need for the African American man to develop a time chart, so that they will become conscience of how they're spending their 24 hours. We will also encourage them so that when they cannot find work, they need to use their time to either acquire a skill or volunteer in an area where they can learn one.

Talent Identification and Development

In the earlier book entitled, *Motivating and Preparing Black Youth to Work*, I indicated that many people will never find their talents. It is important in this area that their counselor or a concerned adult encourage males to find out where their interests and strengths are, and to match careers with their related interest. I want to stress that talents are not just in sports and music, but are also in reading, writing, language arts, computer skills, the ability to concentrate, eye hand coordination, visual, creative, mechanical, etc.

Diet and Nutrition

African American males probably have the worst diet in America. They smoke more cigarettes, drink more liquor, use more hard drugs, eat less fruit and salad, and consume more fried foods, and red meat. In this section, we need to teach African American men how to reduce their red meat intake, consume more natural products, drink more water, exercise and stay away from nicotine, caffeine, and hard drugs. When Malcolm was released from prison, rumor has it that he was so disciplined that he never chewed gum or ate candy anymore from that point.

Economics

This is a very important area, especially for this age group because history and culture alone are not going to be effective, we cannot provide men employment. One of the major reasons for the success of the Nation of Islam other than introducing the males to God, is giving them 300 newspapers, fish, bean pies, and power products to sell. As much as I dislike the drug dealer, he can be credited with providing jobs in our community, while the Black middle class works for someone else. We need African Americans that will create jobs in our neighborhoods. We are not going to save this age group without providing them with the means of employment. There are only two ways of doing it, ASKING the government to provide a national job bill and/or PROVIDING the jobs in our community ourselves by spending 300 billion dollars with each other.

Peer Group and Joining an Organization

When you allow anyone to have bad habits for 18 or 25 years, it is very difficult to break those traits by themselves. I often tell youth that the most important decision of their lives will be the friends they choose. I advocate that the group that you *spend* time with will be the group that you *end* up with and it will shape your personality. Therefore, a very easy way to become successful is to choose positive friends and organizations. Unfortunately, the gangs don't receive an enormous

amount of competition from other groups in the community. The combination of their materialistic possessions and the lack of competition has allowed the gangs to become successful. I'd like to offer this theoretical paradigm that addresses the conspiracy to destroy Black boys.
First, What is the *problem*?
Second, What *caused* the problem?
Third, What are the *solutions*?
Fourth, How can they be *implemented*?
In a typical one hour workshop, you receive 55 minutes of the problem, 4 minutes for causes, 1 minute for solutions, and no time for implementation.

The Problem
At birth there are 1.03 Black boys born into the world to 1.00 Black girls. By the year 2000, 70 percent of all Black male will be unavailable to Black women. 85 percent of the African American children that are placed in special education are African American males; 609,000 African American males are involved in the penal institution; 47 percent of the penal population is African American, and we're only 3.5 percent of the college students. We are 37 percent of the schools suspensions. We have the lowest life expectancy. We have the highest homicide and cancer rates, and 31 percent of the African American males between 18-25 are unemployed. (This is a very conservative figure; some people feel that it's closer to 40 to 45 percent.)

The Causes
White Male Supremacy/Institutional Racism
A Capital Intensive Economy
Drugs
The Male Socialization Process
Double Child Rearing Standards Among Parents
Parental Apathy
Low Teacher Expectations
Lack of Understanding the Male Learning Styles
Negative Peer Pressure and Gangs
The Lack of Positive Male Role Models

Solutions

In order to correct the problems, the solutions have to address the causes.

RACISM—We must understand and resist it, and empower our community to reach it's full potential.

HIGH TECH ECONOMY—A Federal Jobs bill, a reduction in the defense budget and more monies allocated for education and training, a reduction on foreign imports and Black economic development.

DRUGS—We must patrol our borders, enhance self-esteem, not allow stores to sell drug paraphernalia, use the money from drug busts for community programs, allocate more money for treatment, and increase community watch groups.

MALE SOCIALIZATION PROCESS—Increase Rites of Passage programs, produce programs for electronic media portraying Black males strengths, mentally and spiritually.

PARENTAL DOUBLE STANDARD—We must have workshops and books for parents that inform them of the necessity to teach their sons and daughters to be equally responsible and self-sufficient.

PARENTAL APATHY—We must market PTA to attract parents, increase the number of families receiving services from Chapter One and Headstart, provide more workshops.

LOW TEACHER EXPECTATIONS—Mandatory inservice training on expectations from africentric educational scholars.

LEARNING STYLES—Mandatory in-service training using books that explain the specifics of boys and girls maturing at different rates and children of different races often having different learning styles. A moratorium on special ed placement for Black boys, a Black male classroom, attracting more Black male teachers to the classroom.

NEGATIVE PEER PRESSURE AND GANGS—Programs that teach boys the distinction between battles and wars, conflict management, and teach parents how to monitor the peer group.

LACK OF MALE ROLE MODELS—A media campaign showing Cub Scouts, classroom teachers, and other role models all being female and its dire consequences on Black male development.

In conclusion, lets return back to our 7 barometers that we're using to measure how successful we are at developing Black boys to be men. Lets now look at our 18 to 25 year old group and ask ourselves, What is their relationship with God? Are they committed to the race? Do they value academic achievement? Do they have the same esteem in school that they have on the streets? How much time do they spend with their friends? Do they respect elders? Are they responsible now at the age of 18 to 25 for themselves, mates and children?

If you're not satisfied with your answers, its time to implement, "Let's get busy".

Footnotes
Preface

1. Marc Mauer, "Young Black Men and the Criminal Justice System", Chicago, Tribune March 4, 1990, Section 4 p.3.

2. Thomas Parham and Roderick McDavis, "Black Men, An Endangered Species", Journal of Counseling and Development, September 1987, p. 25.

Chapter I

1. Direct Interview National Center for Health Statistics, July 5, 1990.

2. Reginald Jones, "Black Adolescents" (Berkley: Cobb & Henny, 1989), pp. 342-345.

3. Amos Wilson, "Developmental Psychology of the Black Child" (New York: Africana Research Publications, 1978), p. 46.

4. Diane McGuinness, "When Children Don't Learn" (New York: Basic Books) p. 47.

5. Ibid p. 21.

6. Ibid pp. 77-78.

7. Jawanza Kunjufu, "Developing Positive Self-Images and Discipline in Black Children" (Chicago: African American Images 1984), pp. 38-39.

8. McGuiness, op cit, pp. 190-192.

9. Ray Rist, "Student Social Class and Teacher Expectations", Harvard Educational Review, Volume 40, No. 3, August 1970 pp. 411-449.

10. Kunjufu, op cit, p. 17.

Chapter II

1. Antoine Garibaldi, *Educating Black Male Youth*, New Orleans Public Schools, 1989.

2. Janice Hale Benson, *Black Youth Christian Education Conference* Keynote Address Detroit, Michigan April 6-7.

Chapter III

1. Ray Raphael, "The Men From the Boys" (Lincoln: University of Nebraska Press 1988), p. XI.

Chapter IV

1. Thomas Parham and Roderick McDavis, "Black Men, An Endangered Species", Journal of Counseling and Development, September 1987, p. 25.

2. Jewelle Taylor Gibbs Edited, "Young, Black, and Male in American" (Dover: Auburn House 1988), p. 64.

PLEDGE ON BLACK MANHOOD

I am the Black man
Some know me as Imhotep, Ramses,
        Martin or Malcolm.
Others know me as the brother on the corner
        or in jail.

I am both, Detroit Red and Malcolm.
From this day forward, I pledge my life
        to the liberation of my people.
I will put God first in my life.
Black women will feel safe when they see me.
I will be a supportive, responsible,
        and loving husband.
I will hug, talk and listen to, and
        educate my children.
I will be involved in the Scouts,
Role Model and Rites-of-Passage.

Why?
Because I am the Black man — the original man,
        the one and only.
The one that other men are afraid of,
        because they know whenever
        I've seized the opportunity — I succeed.

JAWANZA KUNJUFU